Grammar and Writing 5

Student Workbook

Second Edition

Christie Curtis

Mary Hake

Houghton Mifflin Harcourt Publishers, Inc.

Grammar and Writing 5

Second Edition

Student Workbook

Copyright © 2014 by Houghton Mifflin Harcourt Publishing Company and Mary E. Hake and Christie Curtis

All rights reserved. No part of this work may be reproduced or transmitted in any form or by any means, electronic or mechanical, including photocopying or recording, or by any information storage and retrieval system, without the prior written permission of the copyright owner unless such copying is expressly permitted by federal copyright law. Requests for permission to make copies of any part of the work should be addressed to Houghton Mifflin Harcourt Publishing Company, Attn: Contracts, Copyrights, and Licensing, 9400 Southpark Center Loop, Orlando, Florida 32819-8647.

This edition is based on the work titled *Grammar and Writing 5* © 2006 by Mary E. Hake and Christie Curtis and originally published by Hake Publishing.

Printed in the U.S.A.

ISBN 978-0-544-04424-1

7 8 9 10   2266   22 21 20 19 18

4500697457   B C D E F G

Contents

More Practice and Corny Chronicles

Introduction

People can share their thoughts, ideas, and feelings with others by signing, speaking, singing, drawing pictures, taking photographs, making faces, or writing. You might think of other ways as well, but one of the most common ways for people to communicate is through writing.

You have much to communicate. No two people are exactly alike. There is not another *you* on Earth. Your thoughts and experiences are not exactly the same as anyone else's, so you have unique ideas to share with others. Writing is a good way to do that, for it allows you to record your ideas and memories and save them for the future, maybe even for future generations.

Good writing is a skill; it takes practice just as any other skill does. A masterful musician practices every day, and so does an excellent basketball player. In *Grammar and Writing 5*, you will practice recording your thoughts and ideas on paper to improve your skill.

Writing journal entries will give you daily practice. In addition, the following writing lessons will help you to develop good sentences, strong paragraphs, and well-organized, cohesive essays. You will learn to write clearly and effectively, which is an important lifetime skill.

One of the most important tools that you will need is a **small notebook or card file** for collecting ideas; for jotting down questions or things that you notice; for saving your memories and dreams; and for writing down favorite words, names, and catchy phrases from things that you read or hear. You might even keep drawings, photos, or newspaper clippings in your notebook. This is a place to keep bits and pieces that you might someday use in a poem, essay, or story. You will carry this small notebook or card file with you *everywhere* and make notes in it often.

In addition to your small notebook or card file, you will need a **three-ring binder** for keeping your daily journals and your writing assignments from this packet. Your three-ring binder will help you to organize your work so that you can easily refer back to earlier assignments when necessary.

LESSON 1

The Sentence

The Sentence We have learned that a **sentence** expresses a complete thought. Good sentences are the building blocks of effective writing. A good sentence can be long or short. A long sentence is not necessarily better than a short one.

Our writing goal is not to fill up a page with many words. Instead, our goal is to write clearly so that a reader says, "Aha, I see. I understand what you wrote." Too many words can confuse or bore a reader. A skillful writer makes every word count.

In this lesson, we shall practice writing sentences in which every word adds important information without being repetitive. We can do this two different ways: (1) by combining two or more sentences into one compact sentence and (2) by writing a wordy sentence another way.

Combining Sentences Sometimes combining the information from two or more sentences can reduce the number of unnecessary words in our writing. Consider the sentences below.

WORDY: Ted has red hair. Ted has blue eyes.

BETTER: Ted has red hair and blue eyes.

WORDY: Ted is my friend. Ted plays soccer.

BETTER: My friend Ted plays soccer.

WORDY: Ted swam. Pam swam. I did, too.

BETTER: Ted, Pam, and I swam.

WORDY: My cat eats fish. It eats liver. It also eats grass.

BETTER: My cat eats fish, liver, and grass.

Example 1 Combine information from the two sentences below to make one sentence.

Ted likes soccer. Ted also likes baseball.

Instead of repeating "Ted likes," we put all the information into one compact sentence:

Ted likes soccer and baseball.

Example 2   Combine information from the two sentences below to make one sentence.

My cat is Siamese. My cat chases crows.

Instead of repeating "My cat," we put all the information into one compact sentence:

My Siamese cat chases crows.

Writing It Another Way   Sometimes there is a shorter, more direct way to write a sentence. Consider the following sentence:

The car is washed by Mel.

In the sentence above, Mel does the action. He washes the car. Yet, Mel is not the subject of the sentence. We find him at the end of the sentence. Instead "car" is the subject, but "car" does not act. It is only acted upon; it is washed by someone. We call this passive voice.

Whenever possible, it is better to write a sentence in which the subject does the action (active voice), as in the sentence below.

Mel washes the car.

Compare the sentence pairs below.

WORDY: A crow was caught by my Siamese cat.
BETTER: My Siamese cat caught a crow.

WORDY: The crow has been injured by a cat.
BETTER: A cat has injured the crow.

WORDY: They were tutored in English by Ms. Hoo.
BETTER: Ms. Hoo tutored them in English.

WORDY: She had been amazed at the beautiful sunset.
BETTER: The beautiful sunset had amazed her.

Example 3   Rewrite the sentence below in a shorter, more direct way. Use the active voice.

The window was broken by a baseball.

If we turn the sentence around, putting the last part first, we can make a more compact sentence in which the subject does the action:

A baseball broke the window.

Example 4 Rewrite the sentence below in a shorter, more direct way. Use the active voice.

He has been encouraged by his friends.

If we turn the sentence around, putting the last part first, we can make a more compact and direct sentence:

His friends have encouraged him.

Practice For a–c, combine sentences to make one compact sentence.

a. Jalana is my neighbor. Jalana has a vegetable garden.

_____

b. She grows squash. She grows tomatoes. She grows beans.

_____

c. That tomato is ripe. That tomato will taste delicious.

_____

For d–f, rewrite the sentence in a shorter, more direct way. Use the active voice. (Hint: Put the last part of the sentence first.)

d. They were confused by the question.

_____

e. Max had been startled by the loud noise.

_____

f. The loud noise was made by a dump truck.

_____

LESSON 2

The Paragraph, Part 1

The Paragraph A **paragraph** is a group of sentences that builds on a main idea, or topic. A good paragraph presents one main idea and develops it with additional sentences giving more specific information about that main idea.

The Topic Sentence The **topic sentence** is a complete sentence telling the main idea of a paragraph. Often the topic sentence is the first sentence of a paragraph, but not always. Topic sentences are underlined in the paragraphs below.

<u>Kim's favorite color is turquoise</u>. Today she is wearing a turquoise shirt that matches her turquoise book bag. Yesterday she wore turquoise pants and socks. After saving enough money, Kim plans to buy the turquoise shoes that she saw in a department store.

Before he left home this morning, Phil took out the trash and fed the dog. After school he will fold clean laundry and put it away. Later he will wash and dry the dishes. <u>Phil helps out at home as much as he can</u>.

Example 1 Underline the topic sentence in the following paragraph:

Along Maine's jagged coastline, forests of pine and other evergreen trees grow close to the Atlantic shore. Here you can visit lighthouses that have guided sailors for many years. You might see some people catching lobsters and others picking wild berries. There are many things to see in Maine.

The paragraph above is all about things to see in Maine. Therefore, we underline the topic sentence as follows:

Along Maine's jagged coastline, forests of pine and other evergreen trees grow close to the Atlantic shore. Here you can visit lighthouses that have guided sailors for many years. You might see some people catching lobsters and others picking wild berries. **<u>There are many things to see in Maine</u>**.

Example 2   The paragraph below contains a sentence that does not support the topic sentence. Read the paragraph carefully. Then draw a line through the sentence that does not belong.

Dan has become familiar with the Jerusalem cricket. Yesterday he found a huge, ugly black-and-orange bug on the sidewalk. His brother called it a potato bug, but Dan discovered that a potato bug is also called a Jerusalem cricket. Dan had pizza for dinner. He learned that these bugs are not poisonous and that they spend most of their time underground, eating plant materials.

We see that the paragraph above is all about Dan learning things about Jerusalem crickets. That Dan had pizza for dinner has nothing to do with the Jerusalem cricket topic, so we cross out the sentence as follows:

Dan has become familiar with the Jerusalem cricket. Yesterday he found a huge, ugly black-and-orange bug on the sidewalk. His brother called it a potato bug, but Dan discovered that a potato bug is also called a Jerusalem cricket. ~~Dan had pizza for dinner.~~ He learned that these bugs are not poisonous and that they spend most of their time underground, eating plant materials.

Practice and Review   For paragraphs a–c, underline the topic sentence.

a.   Peter painted his bicycle blue with yellow stripes. Now his friends want him to paint their bicycles the same way. Maggie has asked Peter to paint a peacock on her back fender, for Peter draws beautiful peacocks. Peter is an artist!

b.   People call Michigan the Great Lake State for good reasons. Four huge lakes—Lake Superior, Lake Huron, Lake Michigan, and Lake Erie—surround Michigan's two big peninsulas. These lakes are so gigantic that they almost look like oceans. The name Michigan comes from a Chippewa word meaning "great lake."

c.   I plan to spend this Saturday raking leaves and cutting up fallen branches. Last night's windstorm made a big mess. Besides blowing leaves and branches from trees, it damaged roofs and knocked over lawn chairs, tables, and trash cans. Trash, newspaper, and debris litter the streets.

For paragraphs d–f, draw a line through the sentence that does not belong.

d. I am having a bad day. I woke up late, spilled oatmeal on my shirt, and then stepped in a mud puddle on my way to school. I think I did my homework last night, but I cannot find it in my backpack, so I shall have to do it over again during recess while everyone else is having fun. My cousin rides horses. My hair is a mess, and my socks do not match.

e. Komodo dragons, the world's largest lizards, can grow up to ten feet long. They live on a few small islands in Indonesia. With long, forked tongues and powerful claws, they capture their prey. These scary creatures can run as fast as a dog. Komodo dragons are also excellent swimmers. My friend Jenny used to live on an island.

f. Opossums are a benefit to any area that they inhabit. They eat cockroaches and garden pests, such as slugs and snails. They also eat the overripe fruit that litters the ground. Lemons and oranges are citrus fruits. Resistant to disease, these friendly creatures seldom carry rabies. Constantly grooming themselves, they are almost always clean. Best of all, they are not aggressive and will not attack humans.

For g and h, combine sentences to make one compact sentence.

g. That star is bright. That star is far away.

_____

h. We can identify stars. We can identify planets too.

_____

For i and j, rewrite the sentence in a shorter, more direct way. Use the active voice. (Hint: Put the last part of the sentence first.)

i. Jo was fascinated by Saturn's rings.

_____

j. Sergio's humor is appreciated by most people.

_____

LESSON 3

The Paragraph, Part 2

Logical Order We have learned that a paragraph is a group of sentences that builds on a main idea, or topic. A good paragraph presents one main idea and develops it with additional sentences giving more specific information about that main idea. The supporting sentences are arranged in a **logical order.** The paragraph below tells what happened first, next, and last.

> Melissa saw someone juggling three balls and thought it looked like fun. She wanted to learn to juggle, too. First, she would have to find three balls of similar size. She found three oranges under a tree. Next, she would have to practice tossing and catching. She practiced for hours and hours. Now, she is the best juggler that I know!

Sometimes creating a logical order means placing sentences in order of importance, usually ending with the most important point, as in the paragraph below.

> Melissa's ability to make her own clothes is a wonderful asset. It saves Melissa a great deal of money. More importantly, it enables Melissa to wear clothes in the colors, designs, and fabrics that she likes best. Most important of all, making her own clothes allows Melissa to use her creativity, which gives her a feeling of satisfaction.

Example Arrange the sentences below in a logical order to create a good paragraph.

- When Ms. Hahn finally arrived, the puppy leaped into her arms and licked her face.

- Then, he called the owner, a Ms. Hahn, and gave her his address.

- Ben found a frightened, lost puppy on his porch.

- First, Ben checked the puppy's tags and found the owner's phone number.

What happened first? Then what happened? We can number the sentences like this:

4 When Ms. Hahn finally arrived, the puppy leaped into her arms and licked her face.

3 Then, he called the owner, a Ms. Hahn, and gave her his address.

1 Ben found a frightened, lost puppy on his porch.

2 First, Ben checked the puppy's tags and found the owner's phone number.

Now we can arrange these sentences in order to make the following paragraph:

> Ben found a frightened, lost puppy on his porch. First, Ben checked the puppy's tags and found the owner's phone number. Then, he called the owner, a Ms. Hahn, and gave her his address. When Ms. Hahn finally arrived, the puppy leaped into her arms and licked her face.

Practice and Review

a. Read the sentences below. Then number them according to what happens first, next, etc. (Place numbers one through four in the boxes.)

☐ She finds the pump and begins pumping up the flat tire.

☐ When the tire is full of air, Lisa smiles at her success.

☐ Lisa's bike tire is flat, but she thinks she can fix it.

☐ First, she searches through the garage for a pump.

b. Finish writing the paragraph below, adding three or more sentences in a logical order.

> After school, I shall make a delicious sandwich.

First,_____

_____

_____

_____

_____

_____

_____

_____

c. Underline the topic sentence in the paragraph below.

> Idaho has many precious minerals in its soil. Gem collectors treasure the deep purple Idaho star garnet. In addition, Idaho's snow-capped mountains sparkle like jewels in the sunlight. The Gem State is a fitting nickname for Idaho.

d. Draw a line through the sentence that does not belong in the paragraph below.

> My cousin Nancy has many pets. She has two Morgan horses that she rides on the trails. Nancy's house is yellow with white trim. Her three dogs follow her as she rides on the trails, but her two cats and six chickens stay at home, and so do her fish. Each pet has a name, but there are too many for me to recall.

For e and f, combine sentences to make one compact sentence.

e. June has short hair. June's hair is curly.

_____

f. Eagles soar. Eagles land in high places.

_____

For g and h, rewrite the sentence in a shorter, more direct way. Use the active voice. (Hint: Put the last part of the sentence first.)

g. Debby was distracted by Rufus's barking.

_____

h. The magnificent statue can be seen by all the tourists.

_____

LESSON 4

The Paragraph, Part 3

We have learned that a paragraph is a group of sentences building on a main idea or topic. A good paragraph presents one main idea and develops it with additional sentences giving more information about that main idea. In this lesson, we shall learn one way to produce sentences that support a topic sentence.

Supporting Sentences

You can write sentences that support a topic sentence by asking yourself *who, what, when, where, why,* and *how* questions. Suppose you wanted to write a paragraph using the topic sentence below.

Winter is an enjoyable time of the year.

You can ask yourself the following questions:

Who enjoys winter?

What do people enjoy about winter?

When do people enjoy winter?

Where do people have fun during winter?

Why is winter enjoyable?

How can people enjoy winter?

Answering the questions above will help you to think of supporting sentences for your topic sentence. You might write a paragraph like this:

Winter is an enjoyable time of the year. Some people really like cold weather. Others enjoy winter sports such as skiing, ice skating, and hockey. Snow-capped mountains and glistening icicles are beautiful sights that people can see from a window as they sit all warm and toasty in front of a roaring fire.

Example   Consider this topic sentence:

We can improve our math skills.

Write some *who, what, when, where, why,* and *how* questions to get ideas for supporting sentences. Then write a paragraph.

We can ask the following questions:

Who can improve their math skills?

What can we do to improve our math skills?

When can we improve our math skills?

Where can we go to improve our math skills?

Why do our math skills need improving?

How can we improve our math skills?

Answering the questions above helps us to write the following paragraph:

We can improve our math skills. Some people are good at math, but they can still improve. Everyone can improve. Practicing every day, both at home and at school, will make one faster and more accurate at math. Math skills are important because without math, bankers and salesclerks could not count money, engineers could not construct roads and bridges, we would have no computers, and our world would be in a sorry state!

Practice and Review

a. Read the sentences below. Then number them according to what happens first, next, etc. (Place numbers one through five in the boxes.)

☐ Next, he mixes the bananas, sugar, flour, and other things and pours the batter into a baking dish.

☐ He eats the banana bread while it is still hot.

☐ Mark's bananas are too ripe to eat, but he decides that he can use them to make banana bread.

☐ Finally, he places the dish in the oven and bakes the bread for thirty minutes.

☐ First, Mark gathers the ingredients, mixing bowl, and utensils.

b. On the lines below, complete *who, what, when, where, why,* and *how* questions for this topic sentence: **There are many things I like about my home.**

Who _____ ?

What _____ ?

When _____ ?

Where _____ ?

Why _____ ?

How _____ ?

Now, in your mind, answer the questions above to help you finish writing the paragraph below.

There are many things I like about my home.

_____

_____

_____

_____

_____

_____

_____

_____

c. Underline the topic sentence in the paragraph below.

Andrew collects seashells. Two years ago, he brought home a large abalone shell from a California beach. Last summer, he found some sand dollars on the New Jersey shore. Yesterday, he picked up several large clamshells along the coast of Northern Washington.

d. Draw a line through the sentence that does not belong in the paragraph below.

> Elle organized her desk. She separated her math papers from her grammar papers. Then, she made a special folder for her history notes, and she clipped all her writing assignments into a notebook. Elle has a hamster named Trina. After throwing away unnecessary papers, her desk looked neat and uncluttered.

For e and f, combine sentences to make one compact sentence.

e. Elle has a neat desk. Elle has a clean desk.

_____

f. We drove through Colorado. We drove through Kansas. We drove through Missouri.

_____

For g and h, rewrite the sentence in a shorter, more direct way. Use active voice. (Hint: Put the last part of the sentence first.)

g. I was surprised by the gift.

_____

h. Max's cat might be frightened by Rufus.

_____

Additional Practice Write a paragraph using one of the following sentences as your topic sentence, or make up your own topic sentence. Add at least three sentences to support or more fully explain your topic sentence. (Think: Who? What? When? Where? Why? How?)

1. Caring for a pet requires responsibility.

2. There are many things that I can do to help out at home.

3. Eating nutritious food is important.

4. I have fun with my friends.

LESSON 5

The Essay: Three Main Parts

We have learned that a paragraph is a group of sentences that build on a main idea, or topic.

The Essay An **essay** is a group of paragraphs that build on one main idea. In this lesson, we shall learn about the structure of an essay.

An essay has three main parts:

1. Introductory Paragraph

2. Body or Support Paragraphs

3. Concluding Paragraph

Below is a chart that shows the structure of the typical five-paragraph essay. Each box represents one paragraph.

Introductory Paragraph

Body Paragraph

Body Paragraph

Body Paragraph

Concluding Paragraph

Example From memory, reproduce the chart showing the structure of a typical five-paragraph essay.

We can reproduce the chart like this:

Introductory Paragraph

Body Paragraph

Body Paragraph

Body Paragraph

Concluding Paragraph

Practice and Review **a.** Read the sentences below. Then number them according to what happens first, next, etc. (Place numbers one through four in the boxes.)

☐ Spencer's homework assignment is to write a mystery story.

☐ Finally, he will begin writing the rough draft of his story.

☐ Then, he will make up some interesting characters for the story.

☐ First, Spencer will think of a mysterious situation.

b. In your mind, answer some *who, what, when, where, why,* and *how* questions about this topic sentence: **I would like**

to learn some new skills. Then write three or more supporting sentences to complete the paragraph.

I would like to learn some new skills. _____

_____

_____

_____

_____

_____

_____

_____

c. Underline the topic sentence in the paragraph below.

   The Austrian Franz Schubert became a famous music composer. When he was a child, he sang in a choir, and he always loved making music. He would write new songs, waltzes, and overtures wherever he was. He would compose music while visiting a friend in the hospital or while walking down a street.

d. Draw a line through the sentence that does not belong in the paragraph below.

   Ting is learning to play the drums. With her two pointer fingers, she practices rhythms on her desk, tapping her foot at the same time. Ting has a bird and two fish. Whenever she has a chance, she uses her neighbor's drum set. But even without real drums, she can practice on a small wood-and-rubber pad.

For e and f, combine sentences to make one compact sentence.

e. Juan has a long-haired cat. It is huge.

_____

f. Ms. Hoo has lived in North Dakota. She has lived in Minnesota. She has lived in New York.

_____

For g and h, rewrite the sentence in a shorter, more direct way. Use active voice. (Hint: Put the last part of the sentence first.)

g. The horse might have been startled by the dog's barking.

_____

h. That waltz was composed by Schubert.

_____

i. From memory, reproduce the chart showing the structure of a typical five-paragraph essay.

LESSON 6

The Essay: Introductory Paragraph

We have learned that an essay has three main parts: (1) the introductory paragraph, (2) the body paragraphs, and (3) the concluding paragraph. In this lesson, we shall learn what makes up the introductory paragraph.

Introductory Paragraph

The **introductory paragraph**, the first paragraph of an essay, introduces the main subject of the essay. It tells what the entire essay is about. The introductory paragraph has two parts:

1. An introductory sentence grabs the reader's interest.

2. A thesis statement tells what the essay is about.

We can now add more detail to our chart showing the structure of an essay:

```
┌─────────────────────────────────────┐
│ Introductory Paragraph              │
│     1. Introductory sentence        │
│     2. Thesis statement             │
└─────────────────────────────────────┘


┌─────────────────────────────────────┐
│ Body Paragraph                      │
│                                     │
│                                     │
└─────────────────────────────────────┘

┌─────────────────────────────────────┐
│ Body Paragraph                      │
│                                     │
│                                     │
└─────────────────────────────────────┘

┌─────────────────────────────────────┐
│ Body Paragraph                      │
│                                     │
│                                     │
└─────────────────────────────────────┘


┌─────────────────────────────────────┐
│ Concluding Paragraph                │
│                                     │
│                                     │
└─────────────────────────────────────┘
```

The thesis statement is underlined in the introductory paragraph below.

> There are many outstanding people in this world, but none are as outstanding as my best friend. <u>My friend deserves praise for three important reasons</u>.

In the introductory paragraph above, the first sentence (sometimes called the "hook") grabs the reader's attention so that he or she will keep reading. The second sentence, the thesis statement, clearly tells the reader exactly what the essay is about: three reasons why the writer's friend deserves praise.

The reader expects to read these three reasons in the body of the essay. Perhaps each of the three body paragraphs will give one reason.

Example 1 Underline the thesis statement in the following introductory paragraph.

> People are always looking for the perfect vacation location, and I have found it! The ideal place on a summer afternoon is my grandparents' backyard, for there I can relax, swim, and play.

We see that this essay will be about the perfect vacation place, which is "my grandparents' backyard." So, we underline the second sentence.

> People are always looking for the perfect vacation location, and I have found it! <u>The ideal place on a summer afternoon is my grandparents' backyard, for there I can relax, swim, and play</u>.

Example 2 Complete the chart showing the structure of an essay. Include what you have learned from this lesson about the introductory paragraph.

We reproduce the chart showing the two parts of the introductory paragraph, (1) the introductory sentence and (2) the thesis statement.

```
┌─────────────────────────────────────┐
│  Introductory Paragraph               │
│      1. Introductory sentence         │
│      2. Thesis statement              │
└─────────────────────────────────────┘

┌─────────────────────────────────────┐
│  Body Paragraph                       │
│                                       │
│                                       │
└─────────────────────────────────────┘

┌─────────────────────────────────────┐
│  Body Paragraph                       │
│                                       │
│                                       │
└─────────────────────────────────────┘

┌─────────────────────────────────────┐
│  Body Paragraph                       │
│                                       │
│                                       │
└─────────────────────────────────────┘

┌─────────────────────────────────────┐
│  Concluding Paragraph                 │
│                                       │
│                                       │
└─────────────────────────────────────┘
```

Practice and Review

a. Underline the thesis statement in the introductory paragraph below.

Almost everybody likes good music. Much great music has come from Germany. Three of the most famous German composers are Johann Sebastian Bach, Felix Mendelssohn, and Robert Schumann.

b. Read the following sentences. Then number them in order of importance (ending with the most important) by placing numbers two through four in the boxes.

[1] Grandfather plays tennis every morning for three reasons.

[ ] More importantly, he enjoys the companionship of other players.

[ ] Most important of all, he knows that tennis keeps him physically fit and healthy.

☐ First, he enjoys the sport—the volleying, serving, and keeping score.

c. In your mind, think of *who, what, when, where, why,* and *how* questions for this topic sentence: **I can do some things to help out at home.** Use the answers to your questions to help you write supporting sentences to complete the paragraph.

I can do some things to help out at home. _____

_____

_____

_____

_____

_____

_____

_____

_____

d. Underline the topic sentence in the paragraph below.

This spring, I shall plant a vegetable garden. First, in a small, eight-by-ten-foot rectangle of land, I shall turn over the soil and remove all weeds. Then, I shall plant six tomato seedlings and make two hills for zucchini seeds. Around the perimeter of the garden, I shall plant onions and carrots. If space allows, I might also plant strawberries.

e. Draw a line through the sentence that does not belong in the paragraph below.

Mr. Shade has planted many trees around his home. On the south side of his property, he has two oak trees, an orange tree, an ash, and an elm. Mr. Shade wears red tennis shoes. On the north side, he has planted a grove of avocado trees and several tangerine trees. Walnut trees line the west fence, and pine trees stand tall on the east side.

For f and g, combine sentences to make one compact sentence.

f. The Komodo dragon has a long tongue. It is forked.

_____

g. Juan is my classmate. Juan plays the violin and the cello.

_____

h. Rewrite the sentence below in a shorter, more direct way. (Hint: Put the last part of the sentence first.)

That apple pie was baked by Aunt Steph.

_____

i. From memory, complete the chart showing the structure of a typical five-paragraph essay.

```
┌─────────────────────────────────────┐
│ _____ Paragraph          │
│   1. _____            │
│   2. _____            │
└─────────────────────────────────────┘

┌─────────────────────────────────────┐
│ _____ Paragraph          │
│                                      │
│                                      │
└─────────────────────────────────────┘

┌─────────────────────────────────────┐
│ _____ Paragraph          │
│                                      │
│                                      │
└─────────────────────────────────────┘

┌─────────────────────────────────────┐
│ _____ Paragraph          │
│                                      │
│                                      │
└─────────────────────────────────────┘

┌─────────────────────────────────────┐
│ _____ Paragraph          │
│                                      │
│                                      │
└─────────────────────────────────────┘
```

LESSON 7

The Essay: Body Paragraphs

We have learned that the introductory paragraph, the first paragraph of an essay, grabs the reader's interest and tells what the entire essay is about. In this lesson, we shall learn about the body paragraphs of an essay.

Body Paragraphs

The **body paragraphs,** or support paragraphs, come after the introductory paragraph and before the concluding paragraph. Body paragraphs prove or explain the thesis statement. They provide examples, facts, opinions, or arguments to help the reader understand that the thesis statement is true.

Topic Sentence

Each body paragraph has a **topic sentence** telling the reader exactly what the paragraph is about. The topic sentence is followed by supporting sentences.

Supporting Sentences

Supporting sentences support, prove, or explain the topic sentence of that body paragraph. At least three supporting sentences are usually needed to make a strong paragraph.

Each body paragraph looks like this:

```
Topic Sentence

    1. Supporting sentence

    2. Supporting sentence

    3. Supporting sentence
```

Now we can add more detail to our chart showing the structure of an essay. To each body paragraph box, we can add the topic sentence and three or more supporting sentences.

Example 1

Reproduce the chart showing the structure of an essay. Add the information from this lesson about body paragraphs.

We reproduce the chart below, adding the topic sentence and three or more supporting sentences to each Body Paragraph.

```
┌─────────────────────────────────────┐
│ Introductory Paragraph               │
│    1. Introductory sentence          │
│    2. Thesis statement               │
└─────────────────────────────────────┘

┌─────────────────────────────────────┐
│ Body Paragraph                       │
│    • Topic sentence                  │
│       1. Supporting sentence         │
│       2. Supporting sentence         │
│       3. Supporting sentence         │
└─────────────────────────────────────┘

┌─────────────────────────────────────┐
│ Body Paragraph                       │
│    • Topic sentence                  │
│       1. Supporting sentence         │
│       2. Supporting sentence         │
│       3. Supporting sentence         │
└─────────────────────────────────────┘

┌─────────────────────────────────────┐
│ Body Paragraph                       │
│    • Topic sentence                  │
│       1. Supporting sentence         │
│       2. Supporting sentence         │
│       3. Supporting sentence         │
└─────────────────────────────────────┘

┌─────────────────────────────────────┐
│ Concluding Paragraph                 │
│                                      │
│                                      │
└─────────────────────────────────────┘
```

Example 2 Using the introductory paragraph below, write a topic sentence for each body paragraph to further develop the thesis statement of the essay.

> People are always looking for the perfect vacation location, and I have found it! <u>The ideal place on a summer afternoon is my grandparents' backyard, for there I can relax, swim, and play.</u>

We can write the following three topic sentences to further explain our thesis statement.

Topic sentence #1: I find my grandparents' backyard very relaxing.

Topic sentence #2: I love to swim in my grandparents' pool.

Topic sentence #3: My grandparents' yard is a great place for playing many different games.

Each of the topic sentences provided can be developed into a body paragraph by adding supporting sentences to further explain the topic sentence. For example, we might develop the first body paragraph like this:

topic sentence → *I find my grandparents' backyard very relaxing.*

supporting sentences { It is a quiet place with tall trees. I like to lie in the hammock, listening to the birds sing and watching squirrels gather nuts. No one bothers me there. I can forget all my worries as I rest in that hammock.

In the body paragraph above, supporting sentences follow the topic sentence to explain how relaxing my grandparents' backyard is.

Practice and Review

a. Write three topic sentences to support the thesis statement in the following introductory paragraph:

There are many outstanding people in the world, but none are as outstanding as my best friend. <u>My friend deserves praise for three important reasons</u>.

(Hint: Think about an outstanding friend of yours. What makes that friend outstanding? Is he or she generous? Helpful? Kind? Hardworking? Skillful at something? Knowledgeable? You might also think, *Who? What? When? Where? Why?)*

Topic sentence #1:_____

_____

_____

Topic sentence #2:_____

_____

_____

Topic sentence #3:_____

_____

_____

b. Now develop one of your topic sentences from Practice *a* into a body paragraph. Add at least three supporting sentences.

_____

_____

_____

_____

_____

_____

_____

_____

_____

_____

c. Underline the thesis statement in the introductory paragraph below.

Many people love the mountains, but I prefer the desert. I like the desert's creatures, the wide-open space, and the hot temperatures.

d. Read the sentences below. Then number them according to what happens first, next, etc. (Place numbers one through four in the boxes.)

☐ Manny liked my horned lizard picture and asked if he could have it.

☐ Yesterday I drew a picture of a horned lizard.

☐ He thanked me for the picture by giving me a new sketch pad.

☐ I gave Manny the picture.

e. Underline the topic sentence in the paragraph below.

> Alaska is the source of many products that people in other states enjoy. Salmon, crab, halibut, and herring all come from Alaska. In addition, Alaska has huge forests that produce timber for building houses. Petroleum products as well as vegetables and dairy products also come from Alaska.

f. Draw a line through the sentence that does not belong in the paragraph below.

> Daniela is preparing for a five-day hiking trip in the High Sierras. First, she will ask a friend to go with her because hiking alone is unsafe. Her uncle will loan her a backpack and a pup tent, and she will borrow her cousin's sleeping bag. Daniela needs to plan her meals, purchase some food, and plan her route. Daniela collects postage stamps.

For g and h, combine sentences to make one compact sentence.

g. The hens laid six eggs. The eggs were big and brown.

_____

h. John is my cousin. John plays the guitar.

_____

i. Rewrite the sentence below in a shorter, more direct way. Use the active voice. (Hint: Put the last part of the sentence first.)

The potatoes are peeled by Ron and Susan.

_____

j. From memory, complete the chart showing the structure of a typical five-paragraph essay.

```
┌─────────────────────────────────────────┐
│  _____ Paragraph              │
│     1. _____         │
│     2. _____         │
└─────────────────────────────────────────┘

┌─────────────────────────────────────────┐
│  _____ Paragraph              │
│     _____ sentence            │
│     1. _____ sentence         │
│     2. _____ sentence         │
│     3. _____ sentence         │
└─────────────────────────────────────────┘

┌─────────────────────────────────────────┐
│  _____ Paragraph              │
│     _____ sentence            │
│     1. _____ sentence         │
│     2. _____ sentence         │
│     3. _____ sentence         │
└─────────────────────────────────────────┘

┌─────────────────────────────────────────┐
│  _____ Paragraph              │
│     _____ sentence            │
│     1. _____ sentence         │
│     2. _____ sentence         │
│     3. _____ sentence         │
└─────────────────────────────────────────┘

┌─────────────────────────────────────────┐
│  _____ Paragraph              │
│                                          │
└─────────────────────────────────────────┘
```

The Essay: Concluding Paragraph

We have learned about the first two main parts of an essay, the introduction and the body. In this lesson, we shall learn about the third and final main part of an essay, the conclusion.

Concluding Paragraph The **concluding paragraph** is the final paragraph of an essay. It summarizes the ideas expressed in the body of the essay. The concluding paragraph has three important parts:

1. A restatement of the thesis statement

2. A reference to each topic sentence

3. A clincher sentence (last one)

Your "last words" will leave a lasting impression on your readers.

Notice how the concluding paragraph below refers to the three topic sentences in Example 2 of Lesson 7.

Topic sentence #1: I find my grandparents' backyard very <u>relax</u>ing.

Topic sentence #2: I love to <u>swim</u> in my grandparents' pool.

Topic sentence #3: My grandparents' yard is a great place for playing many different <u>games</u>.

CONCLUDING PARAGRAPH:

restatement of thesis ⟶ In conclusion, there is no better vacation spot than my grandparents' backyard. There, I can relax, swim, and play games. I would rather be there than anyplace else in the world!

reference to each topic sentence

clincher (last sentence)

We see that the concluding paragraph above restates the thesis and contains a reference to each topic sentence. It sums up all the main ideas in the essay and ends with a strong statement. The last words will leave a lasting impression on the reader.

Example 1   Write a concluding paragraph for an essay with the following thesis statement and topic sentences:

> Thesis statement: My friend deserves praise for three important reasons.
>
> Topic sentence #1: My friend Tina helps others.
>
> Topic sentence #2: Tina hardly ever complains.
>
> Topic sentence #3: Tina tries harder than anyone else I know.

Based on the thesis statement and topic sentences above, we can write a concluding paragraph like this:

> **In conclusion, my friend Tina is very praiseworthy. She helps other people, rarely complains, and tries hard in everything she does. I am proud to know Tina, for she is an amazing person.**

Example 2   On the next page, complete the chart showing the structure of an essay. Include the three important parts of a concluding paragraph.

We reproduce the chart below, adding the three important parts of the concluding paragraph.

```
┌─────────────────────────────────────┐
│ Introductory Paragraph               │
│     1. Introductory sentence         │
│     2. Thesis statement              │
└─────────────────────────────────────┘

┌─────────────────────────────────────┐
│ Body Paragraph                       │
│  •Topic sentence                     │
│     1. Supporting sentence           │
│     2. Supporting sentence           │
│     3. Supporting sentence           │
└─────────────────────────────────────┘
┌─────────────────────────────────────┐
│ Body Paragraph                       │
│  •Topic sentence                     │
│     1. Supporting sentence           │
│     2. Supporting sentence           │
│     3. Supporting sentence           │
└─────────────────────────────────────┘
┌─────────────────────────────────────┐
│ Body Paragraph                       │
│  •Topic sentence                     │
│     1. Supporting sentence           │
│     2. Supporting sentence           │
│     3. Supporting sentence           │
└─────────────────────────────────────┘

┌─────────────────────────────────────┐
│ Concluding Paragraph                 │
│     1. Restatement of thesis         │
│     2. Reference to each             │
│        topic sentence                │
│     3. Clincher sentence             │
└─────────────────────────────────────┘
```

Practice and Review   a.   Write a concluding paragraph based on the thesis statement "My friend deserves praise for three important reasons" and the three topic sentences that you wrote for Lesson 7.

_____

_____

_____

_____

_____

_____

b. Underline the thesis statement in the introductory paragraph below.

   The choices that we make today will affect the rest of our lives. We all can make changes for the better in our lifestyles. I would like to improve my study skills, my nutrition, and my sleeping habits.

c. Read the sentences below. Then number them according to what happens first, next, etc. (Place numbers one through four in the boxes.)

☐ Melody puts food in her dog's dish.

☐ Now the contented dog is quiet; he is no longer barking.

☐ Melody's dog is barking because he is so hungry.

☐ The dog gobbles up all the food.

d. Underline the topic sentence in the paragraph below.

   Norman feels irritable today. His socks keep sliding down into his shoes when he walks, and his hair keeps flopping into his eyes. He does not like the annoying sound the heater makes, and his chair is uncomfortable. If his teacher gives one more assignment, he thinks that he will explode!

e. Draw a line through the sentence that does not belong in the paragraph below.

   Alba started today with a smile. She made a new friend, and her long-time friend Yoli complimented Alba on her cheerful attitude. Pigeons come in many colors. Alba passed the math test and finished her homework before school was over. Alba had a good day.

For f and g, combine sentences to make one compact sentence.

f. Dr. Ledfoot drives a red truck. Dr. Ledfoot's truck is small.

g. Lucy has brown hair. It is straight.

_____

h. Rewrite the sentence below in a shorter, more direct way. Use active voice. (Hint: Put the last part of the sentence first.)

These toys are assembled by machines.

_____

i. From memory, complete the chart showing the structure of a typical five-paragraph essay.

```
┌─────────────────────────────────────┐
│ _____ Paragraph              │
│  1. _____          │
│  2. _____          │
└─────────────────────────────────────┘
   ┌─────────────────────────────────────┐
   │ _____ Paragraph              │
   │      _____ sentence          │
   │  1. _____ sentence           │
   │  2. _____ sentence           │
   │  3. _____ sentence           │
   └─────────────────────────────────────┘
      ┌─────────────────────────────────────┐
      │ _____ Paragraph              │
      │      _____ sentence          │
      │  1. _____ sentence           │
      │  2. _____ sentence           │
      │  3. _____ sentence           │
      └─────────────────────────────────────┘
         ┌─────────────────────────────────────┐
         │ _____ Paragraph              │
         │      _____ sentence          │
         │  1. _____ sentence           │
         │  2. _____ sentence           │
         │  3. _____ sentence           │
         └─────────────────────────────────────┘

   ┌─────────────────────────────────────┐
   │ _____ Paragraph              │
   │  1. Restatement of _____         │
   │  2. Reference to each _____         │
   │     _____          │
   │  3. _____          │
   └─────────────────────────────────────┘
```

The Essay: Transitions

We have learned what is contained in an essay's three main parts—the introductory paragraph, the body paragraphs, and the concluding paragraph. Now we can write a well-organized essay, yet our essay will be even better if we add **transitions** to connect paragraphs.

Transitions

A **transition** is a word, phrase, or clause that links one subject or idea to another. We place transitions at the beginning of paragraphs to help the essay "flow" from one paragraph to another. Transitions make the ideas easier for the reader to follow. Here are some typical transitions:

Furthermore,…	*Moreover,…*
On the other hand,…	*Aside from…*
Despite all that,…	*Instead,…*
In short,…	*Finally,…*
As a result,…	*Consequently,…*
Another thing…	*For example,…*
The second reason…	*Generally,…*
A final thing…	*Specifically,…*
In addition,…	*Likewise,…*
In conclusion,…	

Transitions like these tell the reader

- that you are starting to support your thesis statement
- that you are going to bring up a new point
- that you are going to continue giving more information
- that you are about to conclude your essay

Transitional words and phrases can appear anywhere in a sentence.

> *Dad, **too**, enjoys playing baseball.*
> *Tennis is a popular sport **as well**.*

Transitions will greatly improve your writing. Generally, you should have a transition at the beginning of every paragraph except for the first paragraph. Transitions linking paragraphs are underlined in the paragraphs below.

> <u>In addition</u>, I like to swim in my grandparents' pool. Sometimes, I swim many laps to see how many miles I can swim. Other times I just float on my back. I also like diving off the board and…

> <u>Another thing</u> I like to do in my grandparents' yard is to play games. My grandfather has taught me to play croquet and badminton…

Example   Underline the transitional words in each sentence below.

(a) Furthermore, I plan to watch less TV from now on.

(b) Melissa made herself a jacket from an old tablecloth, for example.

(c) To sum up, everyone on the team gave their best effort.

We underline transitional words as follows:

(a) **<u>Furthermore</u>**, I plan to watch less TV from now on.

(b) Melissa made herself a jacket from an old tablecloth, **<u>for example</u>**.

(c) **<u>To sum up</u>**, everyone on the team gave their best effort.

Practice and Review   Underline the transitional words in sentences a–c.

a. I read *Moby Dick,* also.

b. Besides that, we washed all the windows.

c. Nora, therefore, would make an outstanding high jumper.

d. Underline the thesis statement in the introductory paragraph below.

> The mayor of my town despises pigeons and wants to get rid of them because of the messes that they make. I disagree. I believe that we should keep the pigeons because of their beauty, their friendliness, and their pleasant cooing sounds.

e. Read the sentences below. Then number them according to what happens first, next, etc. (Place numbers one through four in the boxes.)

☐ She places the finished scarf in a box and wraps it in bright yellow paper.

☐ Using three skeins of blue yarn, Nina knits a fuzzy winter scarf.

☐ With shiny red ribbon, Nina ties a poofy bow on the bright yellow package.

☐ Nina gives the beautifully wrapped gift to her friend Lucy.

f. Underline the topic sentence in the paragraph below.

Last summer, James took magnificent pictures of brown bears catching salmon in Alaska. There, he also captured a gigantic moose with his camera. In addition, James has taken some stunning photographs of wild birds—cardinals, goldfinches, and parrots—from various parts of the United States. James loves to photograph wildlife.

g. Draw a line through the sentence that does not belong in the paragraph below.

In these days, we can communicate by telephone or email, but in the olden days, people often used pigeons to send and receive information. Because they can fly more than thirty miles per hour over long distances, pigeons were the fastest way for people to communicate. Pigeons carried important messages during World War I. Denver is the capital of Colorado. They were the best means of sending messages for many years.

For h and i, combine sentences to make one compact sentence.

h. Ted wrote an essay. It was a long, funny essay.

_____

i. Gia has a turtle. The turtle's name is Oliver.

_____

j. Write the sentence below in a shorter, more direct way. Use active voice. (Hint: Put the last part of the sentence first.)

My wool coat was destroyed by moths.

_____

k. From memory, complete the chart showing the structure of a typical five-paragraph essay.

```
┌──────────────────────────────────┐
│ _____ Paragraph        │
│   1. _____    │
│   2. _____    │
└──────────────────────────────────┘
┌──────────────────────────────────┐
│ _____ Paragraph        │
│     _____ sentence     │
│   1. _____ sentence    │
│   2. _____ sentence    │
│   3. _____ sentence    │
└──────────────────────────────────┘
┌──────────────────────────────────┐
│ _____ Paragraph        │
│     _____ sentence     │
│   1. _____ sentence    │
│   2. _____ sentence    │
│   3. _____ sentence    │
└──────────────────────────────────┘
┌──────────────────────────────────┐
│ _____ Paragraph        │
│     _____ sentence     │
│   1. _____ sentence    │
│   2. _____ sentence    │
│   3. _____ sentence    │
└──────────────────────────────────┘
┌──────────────────────────────────┐
│ _____ Paragraph        │
│   1. Restatement of _____    │
│   2. Reference to each _____    │
│       _____           │
│   3. _____            │
└──────────────────────────────────┘
```

Brainstorming for Ideas

We have learned all the necessary parts of an essay, including transitions. In this lesson, we shall learn how to prepare to write a five-paragraph essay if we are given a thesis statement.

Brainstorming   **Brainstorming** is a method of quickly capturing ideas about a topic or problem. In this lesson, we shall brainstorm for ideas to create supporting paragraphs for a thesis statement. One way to brainstorm is illustrated below.

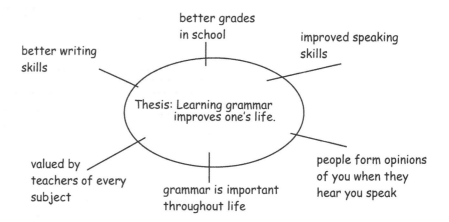

For the next few minutes, use the model above to record brainstorming ideas for this thesis statement: "It is important to protect our environment." You may use the worksheet on the following page. Quickly write in the area outside the circle any and all words that come into your mind as soon as they enter your mind.

- Write quickly. Do not allow your pencil to stop moving.

- Do not worry about spelling or neatness.

- Do not worry about the word order or location.

- Do not think; just write.

Write for about three minutes or until your paper is covered with words, whichever comes first.

When you have finished, you will almost certainly have several ideas to help you get started writing your essay.

It is important to protect our environment.

Organizing Your Ideas

After you have brainstormed, the next step is to examine the ideas that you have generated and identify the ones that best support your thesis statement. Follow these steps to organize your ideas:

1. Take a moment to examine the words or groups of words that you wrote. You will see that some of them relate very well to the thesis, yet others will begin to look as though they do not belong or are not as strong.

2. Choose at least three different words or groups of words that best support the thesis. Circle them. If you cannot decide on just three, you may circle four or five. If you circle more than three words or groups of words, you have more than enough support for your thesis statement. You can write several body paragraphs of support. Or you might later decide to combine one or more arguments or to eliminate the weaker ones.

3. These circled word groups will become your *body paragraph ideas.* Write these ideas on the lines provided below (or type them into your computer file), leaving space underneath each idea to add more notes later for expanding the paragraphs.

4. Look at your *body paragraph ideas* and try to determine the order in which they should be arranged in the body of your essay to best support your thesis. Number the ideas. You can rearrange the order or even eliminate or add additional body paragraphs at any time as ideas come to you.

| # | *Body paragraph idea:* _____ |

_____

_____

_____

_____

| # | *Body paragraph idea:* _____ |

_____

_____

_____

_____

Body paragraph idea: _____

_____

_____

_____

Body paragraph idea: _____

_____

_____

_____

Forming Topic Sentences   Once you have selected the best ideas from your brainstorming and written them on the lines provided, the next step is to take those ideas and form them into topic sentences. Each topic sentence will become a main idea for your essay's body paragraphs.

Practice   Write at least three topic sentences that clearly support your thesis statement. In Lesson 11, we shall expand these topic sentences into body paragraphs and then complete an essay.

Topic sentence: _____

_____

_____

Topic sentence: _____

_____

_____

Topic sentence: _____

_____

_____

Topic sentence: _____

_____

_____

Review Underline the transitional words in sentences a–c.

    a. Furthermore, you need to tie your shoelaces.

    b. Nelly, on the other hand, has missed the bus three times.

    c. George has behaved similarly.

    d. Underline the topic sentence in the paragraph below.

        Kurt is learning to sketch animals. Last year, his horses looked like pigs, but now he can actually draw a horse that looks like a horse. In addition, his pigs now look like pigs. Presently, he is trying to master anteaters and elephants. With practice, he will succeed.

    e. Draw a line through the sentence that does not belong in the paragraph below.

        Karina imagines herself climbing as high as she can in the oak tree out back. She thinks of leaping from rock to rock across rushing rivers. Corn grows in Iowa. If she had wings, she would soar over treetops and land on mountain peaks where wild animals live. Karina loves daring and dangerous activities.

For f and g, combine sentences to make one compact sentence.

    f. The finch had a red head. The finch had a black beak.

    _____

    g. Ms. Hoo is wearing sunglasses. Ms. Hoo's sunglasses are large and round.

    _____

    h. Write the sentence below in a shorter, more direct way. Use active voice. (Hint: Put the last part of the sentence first.)

    Various reptiles were sketched by the young artist.

    _____

i. From memory, complete the chart showing the structure of a typical five-paragraph essay.

_____ Paragraph
1. _____
2. _____

_____ Paragraph
_____ sentence
1. _____ sentence
2. _____ sentence
3. _____ sentence

_____ Paragraph
_____ sentence
1. _____ sentence
2. _____ sentence
3. _____ sentence

_____ Paragraph
_____ sentence
1. _____ sentence
2. _____ sentence
3. _____ sentence

_____ Paragraph
1. Restatement of _____
2. Reference to each _____
   _____
3. _____

LESSON 11

Writing a Complete Essay

In Lesson 10, you brainstormed and created ideas to support the thesis statement, "It is important to protect our environment." You also chose the best of those ideas and put them in the order that best supports the thesis statement. Then you used the ideas to create topic sentences. Now you are ready to write the complete essay.

Practice Using the topic sentences that you wrote for Lesson 10, follow the steps below to complete the essay.

1. For each topic sentence, write a body paragraph to support the thesis statement. To expand your paragraph, you might ask yourself these questions: *Who? What? When? Where? Why? How?* Your answers to these questions will give you ideas for supporting sentences.

2. Create an introductory paragraph with an introductory sentence (a "hook") that will grab the reader's interest and a sentence that states the thesis.

3. Write a concluding paragraph that includes a restatement of the thesis, a reference to each of the topic sentences, and a clincher statement.

4. Add transitions between body paragraphs to make your ideas easier for the reader to follow. Pay special attention to the transition into the concluding paragraph.

5. Finally, put all the parts together to form a complete essay. As you are working, make any necessary corrections to your previous work. You might add or subtract words or make any other change that results in a more effective essay. **Keep this essay in your three-ring binder.** You will evaluate it in the next lesson.

LESSON 12

Evaluating Your Essay

The Writing Process

All of the writing that we do should be viewed as "work in progress." Even after you have turned in an essay to your teacher for a grade, you should not feel that it can never be touched again. The knowledge that *writing is a process* should guide your thinking throughout the construction of an essay. From the first steps in organizing your thoughts, to creating body paragraphs, to adding transitions, you should feel free to make changes to improve your work.

At each step of the writing process, you should stop to reevaluate both your thoughts and the words that you have placed on the page.

It is helpful to do this after each step of the writing process. It is also important to do this after the entire essay is written. In fact, it is probably most helpful to complete an essay, then walk away from it for a day or two, and then come back and read it again.

Many times, sentences that seemed good the first time appear much different a day or two later. Furthermore, you may find that more ideas have come to you or ideas that were somewhat muddled before have become clearer. Two days later, you can write them in a way that is more meaningful to the reader.

Use the following guidelines to help you evaluate your writing.

Evaluating Your Writing

Do not be afraid to change what you have already written. Just because it was typed or written on paper in ink does not mean that it cannot be improved.

Ask yourself these questions throughout the writing process:

- Is my introductory sentence interesting? *If it is not interesting to you, it certainly will not be interesting to the reader.*

- Do I have a thesis statement that clearly explains the subject of this essay? (For this assignment, the thesis was given to you.)

- Does my thesis statement clearly state my position?

- Does each body paragraph have a clear topic sentence at the beginning that tells the reader exactly what the paragraph will be about? *Read each topic sentence without the rest of the paragraph to see if it can stand alone as a strong idea.*

- Are there other sentences that I can add to help improve my credibility and help the reader to better understand my point?

- Have I described my emotions and feelings so well that they create a picture in the mind of the reader to help him or her feel the same as I feel?

- Does each paragraph (except for the first) begin with an effective transition?

- Are there other arguments that I can add as additional body paragraphs to help me prove my point?

- Are some of my arguments weak and unconvincing? Should they be removed because they do not help me prove my point?

- Do my body paragraphs appear in the best possible order to prove my point? Could I place them in a different order that is more logical or effective?

- Is each sentence constructed as well as it should be? *Read each sentence in each paragraph as if it were the only sentence on the page. This helps you to catch sentence fragments, run-on sentences, misspellings, and grammatical errors. If you are working on a computer, put blank lines between each sentence so you actually see only one full sentence at a time on your screen. This will make sentence fragments more visible to you.*

- Does my concluding paragraph summarize and reinforce the ideas and opinions expressed in the essay? Is there a reference to each topic sentence? Is there a clincher sentence?

Practice   Use the Evaluation Form on the following page to evaluate the essay you wrote for Lesson 11. Read your essay carefully as you check for the items listed on the Evaluation Form. Write YES or NO in the blank next to each question.

When you are finished, either you will be confident that you have a strong essay, or you will know where it needs to be improved.

If you answered NO to one or more of the questions on the Evaluation Form, rewrite to improve those areas.

When you can answer YES to every question on the Evaluation Form, you will have completed this assignment.

Essay Evaluation Form

Thesis: _____

_____ Is my introductory sentence interesting? *If it is not interesting to you, it certainly will not be interesting to the reader.*

_____ Do I have a thesis statement that clearly explains the subject of this essay?

_____ Does my thesis statement clearly state my position?

_____ Does each body paragraph have a clear topic sentence at the beginning that tells the reader exactly what the paragraph will be about? *Read each topic sentence without the rest of the paragraph to see if it can stand alone as a strong idea.*

_____ Have I included sentences that improve my credibility and help the reader to better understand my point?

_____ Have I described my emotions and feelings so well that they create a picture in the mind of the reader to help him or her feel the same as I feel?

_____ Does each paragraph (except for the first paragraph) begin with an effective transition?

_____ Are there no other arguments that I can add as additional body paragraphs to help me prove my point?

_____ Are all of my arguments strong and convincing? Do they all help to prove my point?

_____ Do my body paragraphs appear in the best possible order to prove my point? Is their order logical and effective?

_____ Is each sentence structured as well as it could be? *Read each sentence in each paragraph as if it were the only sentence on the page. This helps you catch fragments and run-on sentences and evaluate the overall strength or weakness of each sentence.*

_____ Does my concluding paragraph summarize and reinforce the ideas and opinions expressed in the essay? Is there a clincher sentence?

Supporting a Topic Sentence with Experiences, Examples, Facts, and Opinions

We remember that supporting sentences support, prove, or explain the topic sentence of that paragraph. We have learned to use *who, what, when, where, why*, and *how* questions to come up with sentences to support a topic sentence. In this lesson, we shall discover additional ways to create supporting sentences.

Experiences Your **experiences** or the experiences of other people can strongly support a topic sentence. An experience sentence explains or illustrates an event that supports the topic sentence. Consider the experience sentences below.

> Last winter, I photographed icicles and sparkling frost formations. My framed winter photos now hang on my wall, reminding me that every season is beautiful in its own way.

Examples Like experiences, **examples** can explain or illustrate events that help to prove, support, or explain your topic sentence. Consider the following example sentence:

> For example, snow-covered trees glisten in the moonlight, and the scent of pine perfumes the air.

Facts A **fact** is a piece of information that can be proven to be true. You can use a fact from research to support or prove your topic sentence. Consider the fact sentence below.

> Dr. Bluett's study concludes that winter is an essential season, providing for all living things a time of rest....

Experiences, examples, and facts are always the strongest arguments to prove a point, so they should immediately follow the topic sentence to build a strong paragraph.

Opinions Your **opinions** are your thoughts or feelings about a particular subject. Although a fact is something that can be proven true, an opinion is something that cannot be proven true or false.

For example, it is a fact that Alaska is the largest state in the Union. It is opinion to say that Alaska is the most beautiful state in the Union.

Opinion sentences, communicating thoughts and feelings that are directly related to the topic sentence, may follow experience, example, and fact sentences to further develop the body paragraph. Consider the opinion sentences below.

Shoveling snow and building snow forts can be challenging and fun.

No sport is more exciting than ice hockey.

Ice skating and cross-country skiing are terrific ways to get from here to there.

Example Use experience, example, fact, and opinion sentences to support the following topic sentence:

We have much to learn from older people.

We can write the following sentences to support the topic sentence above.

Experience sentence: My great grandfather recently told me how hard life was during the Great Depression.

Example sentence: For example, my uncle can teach me how to make pizza dough.

Fact sentence: According to Dr. Knowit's most recent study, young people who spend time with people of an older generation know far more about history than young people who spend time only with their peers.

Opinion sentence: I think the best way to learn about the past is to speak with someone who has lived longer than I.

Practice and Review a. Write experience, example, fact, and opinion sentences to support this topic sentence:

If people practice regularly, they can improve their skills.

Experience sentence: _____

_____

_____

Example sentence: _____

_____

_____

Fact sentence: _____

_____

_____

Opinion sentence: _____

_____

_____

Underline the transitional words in sentences b–d.

b. First, he rolled the dough flat, adding flour to keep it from sticking.

c. His hands, shirt sleeves, and pants were powdered with flour as a result.

d. Therefore, he had a big mess to clean up.

e. Underline the topic sentence in the paragraph below.

Tossing small pieces of dry bread crusts into the water, Nels attracts several ducks and geese, which squabble over each tasty morsel. Hungry slider turtles gather around for handouts, too. Then, catfish begin to surface, snatching the bread before the others can get it. Not interested in the bread, a blue heron watches all this and waits for just the right-sized fish to come along. Nels captures the attention of many creatures at the lake.

f. Draw a line through the sentence that does not belong in the paragraph below.

Ms. Hoo has heard many excuses for not turning in homework, but Hargrave's was one of the most creative. Hargrave said that just as he was finishing the assignment, the washing machine overflowed, spewing sudsy water everywhere and soaking his papers. He placed the wet papers outside in the sun to dry. Later, he discovered that they had disappeared. He was not sure, but he thought they now lined the bottom of his neighbor's bird cage. Or, perhaps a Martian had borrowed them. Or, maybe a paper-eating insect had devoured them. Caribou roam the plains of Alaska.

For g and h, combine sentences to make one compact sentence.

g. Tyrell wrote me a letter. The letter was long and newsy.

_____

_____

h. The hungry black bears eat fish. The hungry black bears eat wild berries.

_____

_____

i. Write the sentence below in a shorter, more direct way. Use active voice. (Hint: Put the last part of the sentence first.)

The turtles were fed by Nels.

_____

_____

j. From memory, complete the chart showing the structure of a typical five-paragraph essay.

```
┌─────────────────────────────────────────────┐
│ _____ Paragraph                     │
│    1. _____               │
│    2. _____               │
└─────────────────────────────────────────────┘

┌─────────────────────────────────────────────┐
│ _____ Paragraph                     │
│        _____ sentence               │
│    1. _____ sentence                │
│    2. _____ sentence                │
│    3. _____ sentence                │
└─────────────────────────────────────────────┘

┌─────────────────────────────────────────────┐
│ _____ Paragraph                     │
│        _____ sentence               │
│    1. _____ sentence                │
│    2. _____ sentence                │
│    3. _____ sentence                │
└─────────────────────────────────────────────┘

┌─────────────────────────────────────────────┐
│ _____ Paragraph                     │
│        _____ sentence               │
│    1. _____ sentence                │
│    2. _____ sentence                │
│    3. _____ sentence                │
└─────────────────────────────────────────────┘

┌─────────────────────────────────────────────┐
│ _____ Paragraph                     │
│    1. Restatement of _____                │
│    2. Reference to each _____               │
│       _____                       │
│    3. _____                       │
└─────────────────────────────────────────────┘
```

LESSON 14

Preparing to Write a Persuasive (Argument) Essay

Four Purposes for Writing

Every piece of writing has a purpose. There are four basic purposes for writing: narrative, expository, descriptive, and persuasive.

Narrative writing tells a story or relates a series of events. A composition describing your five-day backpack trip in the Sierras would be narrative writing. In a later lesson, you will write a narrative essay telling about a personal experience of your choice.

Expository writing gives information or explains. An article entitled "How the Railroad Changed America" would be an example of expository writing. Another example was your essay explaining why we need to protect our environment.

Descriptive writing describes a person, place, or thing. Examples include a brochure describing Florida's Everglades, a personal composition about your best friend, and a "Lost Dog" poster that tells exactly what the lost dog looks like. Later you will practice this type of writing by describing a person that you see often.

Persuasive writing attempts to convince someone to do or believe something. An advertisement for Mr. Squeegee's window-washing services, an article about the importance of preserving caribou land, and a campaign flyer urging voters to elect a certain candidate are all examples of persuasive writing. In this lesson, you will write a persuasive essay.

The Persuasive Essay

Keeping in mind the structure of a complete essay, we shall prepare to write a persuasive essay using the following sentence as our thesis statement:

Middle-school students should be required to learn a foreign language.

The goal of this essay will be to convince or *persuade* the reader that middle-school students should be required to learn a foreign language.

Persuasive essays usually deal with controversial topics, subjects that have two sides. If you prefer, you may argue the opposite side and rewrite the thesis statement to read, "Middle-school students *should not* be required to learn a foreign language."

As you do your brainstorming for this exercise, you will discover whether there are enough strong arguments to support your thesis. This is why brainstorming before you write is such an important exercise. It saves you a great deal of time by convincing you that your thesis statement can or cannot be supported, and it gives you the main ideas for all of your topic sentences.

Your essay will prove that your thesis statement is correct. You will use several arguments to convince the reader of this.

Brainstorming

Brainstorming is always our first step in writing an essay. Recall that we draw a circle in the middle of a blank sheet of paper. Inside the circle, write the thesis statement. Then quickly begin to write in the area outside the circle any and all words that come into your mind as soon as they come into your mind.

- Write quickly and do not worry about spelling or neatness.

- Write for about three minutes or until your paper is covered with words, whichever comes first.

- As you write, continue to read your thesis statement in the middle of the circle. This will keep you focused.

Organizing Your Ideas

After you have brainstormed, look at the ideas you have generated and identify the ones that best support your thesis statement. Follow these steps to organize your ideas:

1. Take a moment to look at the words or groups of words that you wrote. Some of them will begin to stand out as relating very well to the thesis; they will firmly argue your point and convince the reader. Others will begin to look as though they do not belong or are not as strong.

2. Choose at least three different words or groups of words that best support the thesis. Circle them. If you cannot decide on just three, you may circle four or five. If you circle more than three words or groups of words, you have more than enough support for your thesis statement. You can write several body paragraphs of support, or you might

later decide to combine one or more arguments. You might decide to eliminate the weaker ones.

3. These circled word groups will become your *body paragraph ideas*. Write these ideas on a separate piece of paper, leaving space underneath each idea to add more notes later for expanding the paragraphs.

4. Look at your body paragraph ideas and try to determine the order in which they should be arranged in the body of your essay to best support your thesis. Number the ideas. You can rearrange the order or even eliminate or add additional body paragraphs at any time as ideas come to you.

Forming Topic Sentences Once you have selected the best ideas from your brainstorming and placed them on a separate page, take those ideas and form them into topic sentences. Each topic sentence will become a main idea for your essay's body paragraphs.

Practice Write at least three topic sentences that clearly support your thesis statement. In Lesson 15, you will develop these topic sentences into body paragraphs and then complete the persuasive essay.

Topic sentence: _____

_____

_____

Topic sentence: _____

_____

_____

Topic sentence: _____

_____

_____

Topic sentence: _____

_____

_____

LESSON
15

Writing the Persuasive (Argument) Essay

In Lesson 14, you prepared to write your persuasive essay. By brainstorming, you gathered ideas. You chose the best of those ideas and put them in the order that best supports your thesis statement. Then you used the ideas to create at least three topic sentences. Now you are ready to write the complete essay.

Practice Using the topic sentences you wrote for Lesson 14, follow the steps below to complete the persuasive essay.

1. For each topic sentence, write a body paragraph to support the thesis statement. Refer back to Lesson 13 for different ways to expand a topic sentence into a paragraph. In addition to experience and opinion sentences, you might write definitions, examples, facts, anecdotes, arguments, or analogies that support the topic sentence.

2. Create an introductory paragraph and a concluding paragraph. Remember that the introductory sentence ("hook") should grab the reader's interest and that the "last words" (clincher) of your conclusion will leave a lasting impression.

3. Add transitions between body paragraphs to make your ideas easier for the reader to follow. Pay special attention to the transition into the concluding paragraph.

4. Finally, put all the parts together to form a complete essay. As you are working, make any necessary corrections to your previous work. You might add things, take things out, or make any other change that results in a more convincing, persuasive essay.

Additional Practice (Optional) After you have evaluated your persuasive essay using the guidelines in Lesson 16, you might try writing another persuasive essay on one of the topics that follow. Choose "should" or "should not" to complete your thesis statement.

1. School cafeterias (should, should not) sell candy to students.

2. Dogs and other pets (should, should not) be allowed on public beaches.

3. My school day (should, should not) be shortened by one hour.

4. Mountain lions (should, should not) be allowed to roam free in areas where people live.

5. Students (should, should not) be allowed to wear whatever they want to school.

Evaluating the Persuasive (Argument) Essay

We have learned that all of the writing that we do is "work in progress." The knowledge that *writing is a process* guides our thinking throughout the construction of an essay. From the first steps in organizing our thoughts, to creating body paragraphs, to adding transitions, we constantly make changes to improve our work.

At each step of the writing process, we should stop to reevaluate both our thoughts and the words that we have placed on the page.

Evaluating Your Writing

In Lesson 15, you completed your persuasive essay. Now that some time has passed, you are ready to evaluate it using the following guidelines.

Ask yourself these questions:

• Is my introductory sentence ("hook") interesting? *If it is not interesting to you, it certainly will not be interesting to the reader.*

• Does my thesis statement clearly state my position?

• Does each body paragraph have a clear topic sentence at the beginning that tells the reader exactly what the paragraph will be about? *Read each topic sentence without the rest of the paragraph to see if it can stand alone as a strong idea.*

• Does each of my topic sentences strongly support my thesis statement?

• Are there other personal experiences, facts, examples, arguments, anecdotes, or analogies, that I can add to help improve my credibility and help the reader to better understand my point?

• Have I described in my opinion sentences my emotions and feelings so well that they create a picture in the mind of the reader to help him or her feel the same as I feel?

• Does each paragraph (except for the first) begin with an effective transition?

- Are there other arguments that I can add as additional body paragraphs to help me prove my point?

- Are some of my arguments weak and unconvincing? Should they be removed because they do not help me prove my point?

- Do my body paragraphs appear in the best possible order to prove my point? Could I place them in a different order that is more logical or effective?

- Is each sentence constructed as well as it should be? *Read each sentence in each paragraph as if it were the only sentence on the page. This helps you to find and correct sentence fragments, run-on sentences, misspellings, and grammatical errors.*

- Does my concluding paragraph summarize and reinforce the ideas and opinions expressed in the essay? Have I convinced the reader that my thesis statement is true? Does my essay end with a powerful clincher sentence?

Practice Use the Evaluation Form on the following page to evaluate the persuasive essay you wrote for Lesson 15. Read your essay carefully as you check for the items listed on the Evaluation Form. Write YES or NO in the blank next to each question.

When you are finished, either you will be confident that you have a strong essay, or you will know where it needs to be improved.

If you answered NO to one or more of the questions on the Evaluation Form, rewrite to improve those areas.

When you can answer YES to every question on the Evaluation Form, you will have completed this assignment.

Persuasive Essay Evaluation Form

Thesis: _____

_____ Is my introductory sentence interesting? *If it is not interesting to you, it certainly will not be interesting to the reader.*

_____ Do I have a thesis statement that clearly explains the subject of this essay?

_____ Does my thesis statement clearly state my position?

_____ Does each body paragraph have a clear topic sentence at the beginning that tells the reader exactly what the paragraph will be about? *Read each topic sentence without the rest of the paragraph to see if it can stand alone as a strong idea.*

_____ Are there no other experiences, facts, or examples that I can add to help improve my credibility and help the reader to better understand my point?

_____ Have I described in my opinion sentences my emotions and feelings so well that they create a picture in the mind of the reader to help him or her feel the same as I feel?

_____ Does each paragraph (except for the first paragraph) begin with an effective transition?

_____ Are there no other arguments that I can add as additional body paragraphs to help me prove my point?

_____ Are all of my arguments strong and convincing?

_____ Do my body paragraphs appear in the best possible order to prove my point?

_____ Is each sentence structured as well as it could be? *Read each sentence in each paragraph as if it were the only sentence on the page. This helps you identify sentence fragments, run-on sentences, and the overall strength or weakness of each sentence.*

_____ Does my concluding paragraph summarize and reinforce the ideas and opinions expressed in the essay? Is there a clincher sentence?

LESSON 17

Writing a Strong Thesis Statement • Developing an Outline

The Thesis Statement The thesis statement clearly tells what the entire essay is about. We have practiced writing a complete essay using an assigned thesis statement. In this lesson, we shall practice creating our own thesis statements for assigned topics.

We remember that the thesis statement not only tells the reader exactly what the essay is about but also clearly states the writer's position on the topic.

Brainstorming When faced with an assigned topic, we prepare by brainstorming in order to generate ideas and thoughts.

The first step in brainstorming is choosing your direction. You would not get into a car and just begin to drive, expecting to arrive at nowhere in particular. You need to know where you are going before you pull out of the driveway. In other words, you must think about the topic, choose your direction or focus, and prepare to define what your essay is about.

For example, if the assignment is to write about the qualities that make a good leader, your thesis statement could begin, "The qualities that make a good leader are ..."

After brainstorming about the topic, perhaps you have decided that there are four specific qualities that make a good leader. If so, your thesis statement might be the following:

There are four important qualities that make a good leader.

Practice Below are ten topics that could be given to you as subjects for essays. For each topic, brainstorm briefly. Then write a declarative sentence that could be used as a strong thesis statement for a complete essay.

1. The best things about the state in which you live

_____

_____

2. The qualities that make a true friend

_____

_____

3. Why a person should learn grammar

_____

_____

4. Things that you would change about yourself if you could

_____

_____

5. What you will do differently as a student this year from what you did last year

_____

_____

6. Some ways that you can help others

_____

_____

7. Some events that you will always remember

_____

_____

8. What you can do to improve or maintain your physical health

_____

_____

Developing an Outline An outline can help us to organize our ideas in a logical manner. In this lesson, we shall review the basic outline form and practice developing an outline in preparation for writing future essays or research papers.

Outline Form An outline is a list of topics and subtopics arranged in an organized form. We use Roman numerals for main topics. For subtopics, we use uppercase letters. For a very detailed outline, we use alternating numbers as shown below.

Title

I. Main topic
   A. Subtopic of I
   B. Subtopic of I
      1. Subtopic of B
      2. Subtopic of B
         a. Subtopic of 2
         b. Subtopic of 2
            (1) Subtopic of b
            (2) Subtopic of b
II. Main topic
   A. Subtopic of II...etc.

Notice that we indent subtopics so that all letters and numbers of the same kind are directly under one another. Notice also that we use at least **two subdivisions** (letters or numbers of the same kind) for a category.

Topic Outline An outline may be either a topic or a sentence outline. In a topic outline, each main topic or subtopic is written as a single word or phrase. Below is an example of a topic outline for the first part of an essay about objections to going to bed.

Bedtime Battles

I. Why bedtimes are necessary
   A. To allow body to rest
   B. To feel alert and energetic the next day
II. Why bedtimes are frustrating
   A. Interrupting my activities
   B. Causing me to miss exciting events

Sentence Outline In a sentence outline, each topic is expressed as a complete sentence. Notice how the sentence outline that follows communicates more meaning than the short phrases of the topic outline.

Bedtime Battles

I. Bedtimes are necessary.
  A. We allow our bodies to repair damaged cells and to replenish damaged cells with enough sleep.
  B. Bedtimes allow enough sleep to make us alert and energetic the following day.
II. Bedtimes can be frustrating.
  A. While reading a mystery or playing a game, we have to stop to go to bed.
  B. While in bed, we might miss a phone call or a visit from a friend.

Practice On a separate piece of paper, practice developing an outline by organizing the following set of information in a topic outline. First, look carefully over the list. You will find one main topic (I.) and three subtopics (A., B., C.). The rest of the items will be subtopics or subtopics of subtopics (1., 2., 3.,…). You might begin by circling the main topic and underlining the three subtopics. You may work with your teacher or with a group of students.

Sports

pitcher	set
forward	bat
sports	basketball
jump serve	dribble
diamond	spike
hoop	baseball
mitt	home run
traveling	volleyball
dig	bump pass
catcher	server
layup	bunt
shortstop	free throw

Additional Practice

a. For Lesson 11, you wrote a complete essay containing at least three body paragraphs. Create a topic outline covering the body paragraphs of that essay. Hint: The topic sentence of each body paragraph will become a word or phrase beside a Roman numeral indicating a main topic in your outline. Therefore, your outline will have at least three Roman numerals.

b. For Lesson 15, you wrote a persuasive essay containing at least three body paragraphs. Create a topic outline for this essay.

LESSON 18

Preparing to Write an Expository (Informative) Essay

The purpose of expository writing is to inform or explain. Expository writing tells why or how. The following might be titles for expository essays:

> "How to Use a Thesaurus"
>
> "New Computer Technology"
>
> "Where to Find the Best Tacos"
>
> "Why the Hamster Makes a Good Pet"
>
> "Making a Rug from Fabric Scraps"

A good expository essay is well organized and clear. It might offer an explanation of how something works, information about a specific subject, or instructions for doing something. You may want to include relevant facts, concrete details, quotations, or examples.

In this lesson, we shall prepare to write an expository essay that explains how to plan a birthday party.

Our goal is to write easy-to-follow instructions, which will require a detailed description of the process. Therefore, we shall break down the actions and carefully sequence them in a logical or practical order so that the reader can understand our step-by-step method of planning a birthday party.

Brainstorming In order to generate thoughts and ideas, we shall brainstorm before creating a thesis statement for our *how-to* essay.

- Write quickly and do not worry about spelling or neatness.

- Write for about three minutes or until your paper is covered with words, whichever comes first.

Writing a Thesis Statement Now it is time to state the purpose of your essay in a clear thesis statement. Using the ideas you have written by brainstorming, write a sentence that tells what your essay is about.

Hint: Will you be presenting a certain number of *steps* in your how-to essay? Or, will you be explaining a number of different *parts* of a birthday party that need to be planned? Your thesis statement will reveal your presentation plan.

Organizing Your Ideas After you have written a strong thesis statement telling what your essay is about, look at the ideas that you have generated by brainstorming and identify the ones that best support your thesis statement. Then you might create thought clusters based on the ideas that you generated while brainstorming. You should have at least three of these clusters to create your body paragraphs. Create a topic outline to organize your ideas.

Tone The **tone** of an essay reflects the writer's attitude toward the topic. Your attitude can be formal or informal, sarcastic or straightforward, serious or silly, admiring or critical. An expository essay should be objective, presenting facts rather than opinions. Before you begin writing, you must decide on your tone.

Forming Topic Sentences Once you have decided on your tone, selected the main ideas from your brainstorming, arranged them in clusters, and developed an outline, take your main topics and form them into topic sentences. Each topic sentence will become a main idea for your essay's body paragraphs.

Practice Write a thesis statement and at least three topic sentences that clearly explain your thesis statement. In the next lesson, we shall develop these topic sentences into body paragraphs and then complete the expository essay.

Thesis statement: _____

_____

_____

Topic sentence: _____

_____

_____

Topic sentence: _____

_____

_____

Topic sentence: _____

_____

Writing the Expository (Informative) Essay

In Lesson 18, you prepared to write your expository essay about how to plan a birthday party. By brainstorming, you gathered ideas and wrote a thesis statement. You chose the best of those ideas and put them into clusters. Then you used the main ideas to create at least three topic sentences. Now you are ready to write the complete essay.

Practice   Using the topic sentences that you wrote for Lesson 18, follow the steps below to complete the expository essay.

1. For each topic sentence, write a body paragraph to support the thesis statement. Refer to your notes or outline and use the ideas underneath each Roman numeral to write body sentences that further explain, or expand, each topic sentence.

2. Create an introductory paragraph. Remember that the introductory sentence ("hook") should grab the reader's interest. Your thesis statement will clearly tell what the essay is about.

3. Create a concluding paragraph that refers to each topic sentence in your body paragraphs. Remember that the "last words" (clincher) of your conclusion will leave a lasting impression.

4. Add transitions between body paragraphs to make your ideas easier for the reader to follow. Transitions that indicate order, such as "the first step..." or "the second step...," are appropriate in a how-to essay. Pay special attention to the transition into the concluding paragraph. Look back at Lesson 9 for help with transitions.

5. Finally, put all the parts together to form a complete essay. Use appropriate links to join connected ideas within your essay. As you are working, make any necessary corrections to your previous work. You might add things, take things out, or make any other change that results in a clearer, easier-to-follow expository essay.

Additional Practice   (Optional) After you have evaluated your expository essay using the guidelines in Lesson 20, you might try writing another expository essay on a topic of your choice or on one of these topics:

1. Explain how to play a game, any game that you know how to play.

2. Write an essay giving at least three reasons why you are thankful to be living in the United States of America.

3. Give instructions for making a breakfast that you like.

4. Explain in detail how one might decorate a yard or room for a friend's birthday party.

5. Compare and contrast the octopus and the squid.

6. Tell how to construct a kite, paper airplane, or some other craft of your choice.

7. Compare and contrast the typical personality of a dog and a cat.

8. Explain how three people have positively affected your life.

Evaluating the Expository (Informative) Essay

We remember that all of our writing is "work in progress." The knowledge that *writing is a process* guides our thinking throughout the construction of an essay. Throughout the steps of brainstorming, organizing our thoughts, creating body paragraphs, and adding transitions, we constantly make changes to improve our work.

Evaluating Your Writing

In Lesson 19, you completed your expository essay. Now that some time has passed, you are ready to evaluate it using the following guidelines.

Ask yourself these questions:

• Is my introductory sentence ("hook") interesting? *If it is not interesting to you, it certainly will not be interesting to the reader.*

• Does my thesis statement clearly state what my essay is about?

• Does each body paragraph have a clear topic sentence at the beginning that tells the reader exactly what the paragraph will be about? *Read each topic sentence without the rest of the paragraph to see if it can stand alone as a strong idea.*

• Does each of my topic sentences strongly support my thesis statement?

• Are there other concrete details, facts, examples, or steps, that I can add to help improve my explanation or help the reader to better follow my instructions?

• Have I defined all technical terms and subject-specific vocabulary in my essay?

• Are my sentences in a logical or practical order?

• Does each paragraph (except for the first) begin with an effective transition?

• Are there other details that I can add as additional body paragraphs to create a fuller or clearer explanation?

- Are some of my sentences weak or confusing? Should they be removed because they do not help me to explain?

- Do my body paragraphs appear in the best possible order? Could I place them in a different order that is more logical or effective?

- Is each sentence constructed as well as it should be? *Read each sentence in each paragraph as if it were the only sentence on the page. This helps you to catch sentence fragments, run-on sentences, misspellings, and grammatical errors.*

- Does my concluding paragraph summarize and reinforce the ideas expressed in the essay? Have I written a powerful clincher?

Practice Use the Evaluation Form on the following page to evaluate the expository essay you wrote for Lesson 19. Read your essay carefully as you check for the items listed on the Evaluation Form. Write YES or NO in the blank next to each question.

When you are finished, either you will be confident that you have a strong essay, or you will know where it needs to be improved.

If you answered NO to one or more of the questions on the Evaluation Form, rewrite to improve those areas.

When you can answer YES to every question on the Evaluation Form, you will have completed this assignment.

Expository Essay Evaluation Form

Thesis: _____

_____ Is my introductory sentence (hook) interesting? *If it is not interesting to you, it certainly will not be interesting to the reader.*

_____ Do I have a thesis statement that clearly explains the subject of this essay?

_____ Does my thesis statement clearly state my method of presentation?

_____ Does each body paragraph have a clear topic sentence at the beginning that tells the reader exactly what the paragraph will be about? *Read each topic sentence without the rest of the paragraph to see if it can stand alone as a strong idea.*

_____ Have I included every detail, fact, or example that I can to help improve my explanation and help the reader to better understand my point?

_____ Within each paragraph, are my sentences in a logical or practical order?

_____ Does each paragraph (except for the first paragraph) begin with an effective transition?

_____ Are there no other ideas that I can add as additional body paragraphs to create a fuller or clearer explanation?

_____ Are all of my sentences strong and clear? Do they all help me to explain?

_____ Do my body paragraphs appear in the best possible order? Is their order logical and effective?

_____ Is each sentence structured as well as it could be? *Read each sentence in each paragraph as if it were the only sentence on the page. This helps you identify sentence fragments, run-on sentences, and the overall strength or weakness of each sentence.*

_____ Does my concluding paragraph summarize and reinforce each main idea expressed in the essay? Is there a clincher sentence?

LESSON 21

Preparing to Write a Personal Narrative

Personal Narrative

Narrative writing tells a story or relates a series of events. In a **personal narrative,** the writer tells a story about a significant personal experience or event.

In this lesson, you will prepare to write a personal narrative in which you will share your feelings about how an experience affected you or taught you something.

Since this will be a personal narrative—a story that happened to you—you will be writing in "the first person." Writing in the first person is just as if you were telling one of your friends about something that happened to you at school yesterday. You will be using "I" and "we," and you can include action, suspense, vivid description, and even dialogue.

Choosing a Personal Experience

To think of an experience for a personal narrative that you would like to share, consider the following:

- a wonderful (or disastrous) first time that you did something

- a memorable struggle or hardship that you experienced

- a "turning point" in your life

- an interesting, exciting, humorous, or moving event in your life

- an unusual or once-in-a-lifetime experience, such as touring a distant country, meeting a famous person, or making an amazing discovery

Reading through the daily journals that you have written might give you additional ideas.

Brainstorming

On a piece of scratch paper, quickly write every experience that comes to your mind. When you have finished, select the one that you think is most interesting and write it on another piece of paper.

After selecting the experience you plan to write about in your personal narrative, begin brainstorming in order to recall details or emotions about this experience. List all words and phrases that come to mind. Without concern for spelling or grammar, write everything that occurs to you.

Organizing Your Information Once you have gathered your thoughts and memories, begin to plan your narrative by organizing the events in a logical order, which might be chronological order—the sequence in which the events occurred. Your rough plan might look something like this:

First: I had planted a row of corn in the yard, and…

Then: Crows swooped down and ate the kernels that I had placed in the furrow, and…

Then: I sowed more kernels in the furrow and chased away the crows, and…

Finally: I have learned why farmers put scarecrows in cornfields.

Using Accurate Verbs and Tenses In a narrative essay, we use a variety of verbs and tenses to convey different times, sequences, and conditions accurately. You have learned to use past, present, and future tenses along with helping verbs to create precise meaning (he *must…*, she *might…*, they *should…*, etc.). You have also practiced the four principal parts of both regular and irregular verbs, which are the tools you need to form other verb tenses, such as the **perfect tenses.**

The perfect tenses show that an action has been completed or "perfected." To form these tenses, we add a form of the helping verb *have* to the past participle.

Present Perfect The present perfect tense describes an action that occurred in the past and is complete or continuing in the present. We add the present forms of the verb *have* to the past participle.

PRESENT PERFECT TENSE = HAVE OR HAS + PAST PARTICIPLE

Julie <u>has written</u> her essay.

I <u>have learned</u> a lesson.

| Past Perfect | The past perfect tense describes past action completed before another past action. We use the helping verb *had* before the past participle. |

PAST PERFECT TENSE = HAD + PAST PARTICIPLE

I <u>had planted</u> the seeds already.

Birds <u>had eaten</u> them immediately.

| Future Perfect | The future perfect tense describes future action to be completed before another future action. We add the future form of the helping verb *have* to the past participle. |

FUTURE PERFECT TENSE = WILL HAVE OR SHALL HAVE + PAST PARTICIPLE

Julie <u>will have finished</u> her work by noon.

We <u>shall have written</u> many essays before June.

Notice that we use the past participle and not the past tense to form the perfect tenses:

He <u>has *gone*</u> (not *went*)....

She <u>has *sung*</u> (not *sang*)....

They <u>will have *taken*</u> (not *took*)....

| **Practice** | Following the examples provided, complete the sentences below using perfect tenses. |

1. Rex (past perfect of *eat*) three cookies before dinner.

_____

_____

2. Molly (present perfect of *wear*) that dress two times.

_____

_____

3. By lunchtime, we (future perfect of *plant*) all the seeds.

_____

_____

Practice For your personal narrative, write a rough plan similar to the one on the second page of this lesson. In the next lesson, you will expand each part of this plan into a paragraph and complete your narrative by filling in detail, action, and dialogue. Use a variety of accurate verbs and tenses to make your essay more precise and interesting.

First: _____

_____

Then: _____

_____

Then: _____

_____

Then: _____

_____

Finally: _____

_____

_____

Writing a Personal Narrative

In Lesson 21, you chose an interesting personal experience and created a rough plan for writing a personal narrative. In this lesson, you will use your rough plan and any other notes and begin writing your narrative.

Opening Paragraph Remember that your opening paragraph should capture the interest of the reader and establish your tone, which reveals your feelings or attitudes about the experience. You will write in first person, using the pronoun *I* or *we*.

Body Paragraphs Although you have a plan to follow, you may alter it as you write. Following the opening paragraph, each "then" part of your rough plan might become the topic sentence for a body paragraph in which you fill in details, actions, and any necessary dialogue.

Concluding Paragraph Your concluding paragraph will include a personal summary or commentary about how the experience affected you or taught you something significant.

Practice Write your personal narrative according to the guidelines above. Include an opening paragraph, two or more body paragraphs, and a concluding paragraph.

LESSON 23

Evaluating the Personal Narrative

All of our writing is "work in progress." The knowledge that *writing is a process* guides our thinking throughout the construction of our personal narrative. From the first steps in selecting an experience to share, to organizing our thoughts, to creating body paragraphs, to adding transitions, we constantly make changes to improve our work.

Evaluating Your Writing

In Lesson 22, you completed your personal narrative. Now that some time has passed, you are ready to evaluate it using the following guidelines.

Ask yourself these questions:

• Is my introductory sentence ("hook") interesting? *If it is not interesting to you, it certainly will not be interesting to the reader.*

• Does the beginning of the narrative clearly establish the tone?

• Does each body paragraph have a clear topic sentence at the beginning that tells the reader exactly what the paragraph will be about? *Read each topic sentence without the rest of the paragraph to see if it can stand alone as a strong idea.*

• Is the first-person point of view consistently maintained throughout the narrative?

• Are there other details, descriptions, emotions, or dialogue I could add to make a more interesting narrative?

• Are my sentences in a logical or chronological order? Have I used a variety of time-related terms to order the events?

• Does each paragraph (except for the first) begin with an effective transition?

• Are there other details that I can add as additional body paragraphs to create a fuller or more complete narrative?

• Are some of my sentences weak or confusing? Should they be removed because they do not relate to the story?

- Do my body paragraphs appear in the best possible order? Could I place them in a different order that is more logical or effective?

- Is each sentence constructed as well as it should be? *Read each sentence in each paragraph as if it were the only sentence on the page. This helps you to catch sentence fragments, run-on sentences, misspellings, and grammatical errors.*

- Does my concluding paragraph contain a summary or commentary about how the experience affected me? Is there a clincher sentence?

Practice Use the Evaluation Form on the following page to evaluate the personal narrative that you wrote for Lesson 22. Read your narrative carefully as you check for the items listed on the Evaluation Form. Write YES or NO in the blank next to each question.

When you are finished, either you will be confident that you have a strong personal narrative, or you will know where it needs to be improved.

If you answered NO to one or more of the questions on the Evaluation Form, rewrite to improve those areas.

When you can answer YES to every question on the Evaluation Form, you will have completed this assignment.

Personal Narrative Evaluation Form

Title: _____

_____ Is my introductory sentence ("hook") interesting? *If it is not interesting to you, it certainly will not be interesting to the reader.*

_____ Does the beginning of the narrative clearly establish the tone?

_____ Is the first-person point of view consistently maintained throughout the narrative?

_____ Does each body paragraph have a clear topic sentence at the beginning that tells the reader exactly what the paragraph will be about? *Read each topic sentence without the rest of the paragraph to see if it can stand alone as a strong idea.*

_____ Do the details all contribute to the reader's understanding of my personal experience?

_____ Within each paragraph, are my sentences in a logical or practical order?

_____ Does each paragraph (except for the first paragraph) begin with an effective transition?

_____ Are there no other details that I can add as additional body paragraphs to create a fuller or more complete narrative?

_____ Are all of my sentences strong and clear? Do they all directly relate to the story?

_____ Do my body paragraphs appear in the best possible order? Is their order logical and effective?

_____ Is each sentence structured as well as it could be? *Read each sentence in each paragraph as if it were the only sentence on the page. This helps you identify sentence fragments, run-on sentences, and the overall strength or weakness of each sentence.*

_____ Does my concluding paragraph contain a personal summary or commentary about how the experience affected me or taught me something?

Preparing to Write a Descriptive Essay

Descriptive writing describes a person, place, object, or event. With language that appeals to the senses, descriptive writing creates pictures in the reader's mind. Strong, vivid, and precise words are essential in creating clear descriptions.

In this lesson, we shall discuss the use of modifiers, comparisons, and sensory expressions to create accurate and complete descriptions. Then you will prepare to write a descriptive essay about a person whom you can observe as you are writing.

Modifiers To add detail, we can use modifiers: adjectives and adverbs; phrases and clauses. Modifiers supply additional information, making nouns and verbs more specific and precise.

> *Firmly* but *kindly*, my teacher *carefully* made *many red* marks on my *hastily* written essay.

Comparisons In addition to modifiers, we can use comparisons to make a description more vivid. *Simile* and *metaphor* are two kinds of comparisons. A **simile** expresses similarity between two things by using the word *like* or *as*:

> *Like a lone rooster*, the bully strutted proudly across the playground.

A **metaphor**, on the other hand, describes one thing as though it were another thing:

> Strutting proudly, the bully *was a lone rooster* on the playground.

Both comparisons, simile and metaphor, help the reader to see a fuller picture of the bully on the playground.

Sensory Expressions To create a more vivid image, we can appeal to the reader's five senses by detailing things that one can see, hear, smell, taste, and touch. For example, we can hear a goose *honk,* see a distant light *glimmer,* smell the *noxious odor* of a skunk, feel the *smoothness* of a polished stone, and taste the *sour* lemon that purses our lips.

Below, E. Nesbit uses details, modifiers, and comparisons to describe a scene in *The Enchanted Castle*.

> The wide High Street, even at the busy morning hour almost as quiet as a dream-street, lay bathed in sunshine; the leaves shone fresh from last night's rain, but the road was dry, and in the sunshine the very dust of it sparkled like diamonds. The beautiful old houses, standing stout and strong, looked as though they were basking in the sunshine and enjoying it.

Nesbit uses similes to describe flowers.

> So the carnations were bought, a bunch of yellow ones, like sulphur, a bunch of white ones like clotted cream, and a bunch of red ones like the cheeks of the doll that Kathleen never played with.

In *The Enchanted Castle*, E. Nesbit creates a metaphor.

> Johnson's voice was ponderous as his boots.

Nesbit uses description to create a sensory picture.

> And after a long stretch of turf they passed under the heaped-up heavy masses of lime-trees and came into a rose-garden, bordered with thick, close-cut yew hedges, and lying red and pink and green and white in the sun, like a giant's many-coloured, highly-scented pocket-handkerchief.

The examples above show how an author can create vivid pictures using details, modifiers, comparisons, and sensory expressions.

Correlative Conjunctions

Correlative conjunctions connect elements of a sentence that are equal in form, or parallel. Always used in pairs, they join similar words to words, phrases to phrases, or clauses to clauses. Here we list the most common ones:

both—and	either—or
neither—nor	not only—but also

When used correctly, correlative conjunctions can enhance our descriptions. Equal parts, or parallel elements, are italicized in the sentences that follow.

> Jake felt **not only** *tired and hungry* **but also** *hot and thirsty.*

> **Both** *handsome* **and** *energetic*, Ben captured my attention.

Ginger the cat has **neither** *a fine coat* **nor** *a pleasant disposition.*

Either *Peg is very shy* **or** *she has nothing to say.*

Correlative conjunctions must join similar parts:

No: Rudy is **both** strong, **and** he plays tennis well.
[joins an adjective and a clause]

Yes: Rudy is **both** strong **and** athletic.
[joins two adjectives]

No: **Either** she lost it **or** forgot it.
[joins a clause and a phrase]

Yes: **Either** she lost it, **or** she forgot it.
[joins two clauses]

Yes: She **either** lost it **or** forgot it.
[joins two phrases]

No: Nan likes **neither** jewelry **nor** to get a tattoo.
[joins a noun and a phrase]

Yes: Nan likes **neither** jewelry **nor** tattoos.
[joins two nouns]

Consider using correlative conjunctions to create a more interesting descriptive essay.

Brainstorming After choosing one person whom you can observe as you write, you are ready to begin brainstorming in order to gather precise and concrete details that will appeal to the reader's senses and fully describe that person.

You might want to consider these aspects of the person:

1. Physical appearance: size, age, gender; colors, shapes, and textures of hair, eyes, skin, and clothing; peculiar features or facial expressions; movements and gestures

2. Personality traits: mannerisms, habits, usual disposition. By their actions, people may demonstrate that they are intense or relaxed, active or inactive, outgoing or shy, humble or proud, etc.

3. How the person affects others and the world around him or her: Where does the person live? What does the person do? What are his or her passions or interests? How does he or she relate to others? How does this person make you or other people feel?

On a blank piece of paper, quickly write everything that comes to your mind concerning the person that you wish to describe. Without regard for spelling or grammar, write all the nouns, verbs, adjectives, adverbs, phrases, clauses, comparisons, and sensory expressions that occur to you.

Use reference materials, such as dictionaries and thesauruses, both print and digital, to find additional precise and appropriate words and phrases for your essay.

Organizing Your Information Once you have gathered your thoughts and observations, begin to plan your descriptive essay by grouping the words and phrases into clusters. You might have one cluster of words and phrases that describe the person's physical appearance, another cluster focusing on the person's personality, and another telling about what the person does and how the person affects others and the world around him or her.

You can use each idea cluster to develop a topic sentence for each body paragraph in your essay.

Thesis Statement In your essay, you will be describing many different aspects of one person. What is the main impression you want your reader to receive concerning this person? Your thesis statement will sum up that which is most important.

Practice For your descriptive essay, write a thesis statement and three or more topic sentences about the person that you wish to describe. In the next lesson, you will develop each topic sentence into a body paragraph by adding more detail. Keep your brainstorming paper and this assignment in your three-ring binder so that you will be ready to complete your essay.

Thesis statement: _____

_____

_____

Topic sentence: _____

_____

_____

Topic sentence: _____

_____

_____

Topic sentence: _____

_____

_____

Writing a Descriptive Essay

In Lesson 24, you prepared to write your descriptive essay about a person of your choice. By brainstorming, you gathered ideas and details. Then you organized those details into clusters representing main ideas. From those clusters, you created a thesis statement and at least three topic sentences. Now you are ready to write the complete essay.

Practice Using the topic sentences that you wrote for Lesson 24, follow the steps below to complete the descriptive essay.

1. Develop each topic sentence into a body paragraph, keeping your thesis in mind. Refer to your brainstorming notes and idea clusters to write body sentences that add more detail and create a vivid picture in the reader's mind.

2. Create an introductory paragraph and a concluding paragraph. Remember that the introductory sentence ("hook") should grab the reader's interest and that the "last words" (clincher) of your conclusion will leave a lasting impression.

3. Add a variety of effective transitions between body paragraphs to make your ideas easier for the reader to follow. Pay special attention to the transition into the concluding paragraph.

4. Finally, put all the parts together to form a complete essay. As you are working, make any necessary corrections to your previous work. You might add things, remove things, or make any other change that results in a clearer, fuller descriptive essay.

Additional Practice (Optional) After you have evaluated your descriptive essay using the guidelines in Lesson 26, you might try writing another descriptive essay on a topic of your choice or on one of these topics:

1. A character from a novel you have read

2. A room in your house or apartment

3. A pet, or an animal that interests you

4. An interesting or beautiful outdoor scene

5. A sporting event, birthday party, or other kind of celebration

Evaluating the Descriptive Essay

Because *writing is a process* and all of our writing is "work in progress," we constantly make changes to improve our work.

Evaluating Your Writing

In Lesson 25, you completed your descriptive essay. Now that some time has passed, you are ready to evaluate it using the following guidelines.

Ask yourself these questions:

• Is my introductory sentence ("hook") interesting? *If it is not interesting to you, it certainly will not be interesting to the reader.*

• Does the thesis statement focus on a single person, place, object, or event?

• Does the thesis statement give my main impression of the person, place, object, or event that I am describing?

• Does each body paragraph have a clear topic sentence at the beginning that tells the reader exactly what the paragraph will be about? *Read each topic sentence without the rest of the paragraph to see if it can stand alone as a strong idea.*

• Are there other details, modifiers, comparisons, or sensory expressions that I could add to help the reader to visualize my topic?

• Are my sentences in a logical order?

• Does each paragraph (except for the first) begin with an effective transition?

• Are there other details that I can add as additional body paragraphs to create a fuller or more complete description?

• Are some of my sentences weak or confusing? Should they be removed because they do not relate to the topic?

• Do my body paragraphs appear in the best possible order? Could I place them in a different order that is more logical or effective?

- Is each sentence constructed as well as it should be? *Read each sentence in each paragraph as if it were the only sentence on the page. This helps you to catch sentence fragments, run-on sentences, misspellings, and grammatical errors.*

- Does my concluding paragraph sum up my main impression of the person, place, object, or event?

Practice Use the Evaluation Form on the following page to evaluate the descriptive essay that you wrote for Lesson 25. Read your descriptive essay carefully as you check for the items listed on the Evaluation Form. Write YES or NO in the blank next to each question.

When you are finished, either you will be confident that you have a strong descriptive essay, or you will know where it needs to be improved.

If you answered NO to one or more of the questions on the Evaluation Form, rewrite to improve those areas.

When you can answer YES to every question on the Evaluation Form, you will have completed this assignment.

Descriptive Essay Evaluation Form

Topic: _____

_____ Is my introductory sentence (hook) interesting? *If it is not interesting to you, it certainly will not be interesting to the reader.*

_____ Does the thesis statement focus on a single person, place, object, or event?

_____ Does the thesis statement give my main impression of that person, place, object, or event?

_____ Does each body paragraph have a clear topic sentence at the beginning that tells the reader exactly what the paragraph will be about? *Read each topic sentence without the rest of the paragraph to see if it can stand alone as a strong idea.*

_____ Do the details all contribute to the reader's ability to visualize or mentally experience my topic?

_____ Within each paragraph, are my sentences in a logical order?

_____ Does each paragraph (except for the first paragraph) begin with an effective transition?

_____ Have I used enough modifiers, comparisons, and sensory expressions to enable the reader to visualize my topic?

_____ Are all of my sentences strong and clear? Do they all directly relate to the topic?

_____ Do my body paragraphs appear in the best possible order? Is their order logical and effective?

_____ Is each sentence structured as well as it could be? *Read each sentence in each paragraph as if it were the only sentence on the page. This helps you identify sentence fragments, run-on sentences, and the overall strength or weakness of each sentence.*

_____ Does my concluding paragraph sum up my main impression of my topic? Is there a clincher sentence?

LESSON 27

Writing a Chapter Summary

A summary is a brief restatement of the main idea(s) in something one has read. In a summary, the writer omits details and condenses a long passage—a whole story, chapter, or book—to its main idea(s). Therefore, the summary is much shorter than the original passage.

In this lesson, we shall practice writing a one-paragraph summary of a chapter in a novel.

Chapter Summary If you were reading a novel to a friend, and if your friend fell asleep during one of the chapters, he or she might miss a great deal of the action or storyline. Your brief *summary* of that missing chapter could help your friend to continue quickly to the next chapter without confusion and without rereading the entire chapter.

Example Below is a summary of the first chapter of *Little House on the Prairie,* by Laura Ingalls Wilder. Notice that we use the present tense of verbs.

> A girl named Laura, her parents, and her two sisters leave their comfortable home in the Big Woods of Wisconsin and head West. Laura's Pa thinks there are too many people in Wisconsin. He wants to live in wide-open country where wild animals roam. So the family says goodbye to all its relatives and travels by covered wagon across Minnesota, Iowa, and Missouri to the big, flat, windy prairie in Kansas. The children get very tired on this long journey.
>
> Summary by Peter Cheung

Practice In a single paragraph, summarize one chapter of a novel you are reading or have read in the past (or a novel from the list below). Your paragraph should not exceed 150 words. Your summary should include major characters and provide a sense of what happens in the chapter. Use present tense of verbs.

Suggested novels for this exercise:

The Magic Bicycle, by John Bibee

The Phantom Tollbooth, by Norton Juster

Tuck Everlasting, by Natalie Babbitt

The Bronze Bow, by Elizabeth G. Speare

Old Yeller, by Fred Gipson

The Forgotten Door, by Alexander Key

The Secret Garden, by Frances H. Burnett

Where the Red Fern Grows, by Wilson Rawls

Preparing to Write an Imaginative Story

We have practiced writing vivid descriptions of people, places, objects, or events using details, modifiers, comparisons, and sensory expressions. We have also written a personal narrative with dialogue, logical sentence order, and effective transitions. In this lesson, we shall use all the writing skills that we have learned so far to create our own imaginative story.

An imaginative story is fiction; it is not a true story, although it may be based on something that really happened.

Conflict, characters, setting, and plot are all parts of the imaginative story. In preparing to write our story, we shall gather information concerning each of these parts.

Conflict A short story must have a problem or situation in which struggle occurs. A character may be in conflict with another character, with the forces of nature, with the rules of society, or even with his or her own self, as an internal conflict brought about by pangs of conscience or feelings of confusion.

For example, notice the possible conflicts related to the two situations that follow.

SITUATION 1: Iona does not like her middle name and wants to change it.

Conflict: Some people tease her about her name.

Conflict: Iona's parents gave her that name and do not want her to change it.

Conflict: Iona's grandma feels hurt, for Iona was named after her.

SITUATION 2: Ivan forgets to set his alarm clock to wake him for his basketball game.

Conflict: He does not have time to eat breakfast, so he might not have energy to play his best in the game.

Conflict: He has missed the bus and does not know how he will get to the game.

Conflict: His team might have to forfeit the game,

for they will not have enough players.

To find a situation and conflict for your own imaginative story, you might talk to friends or family members, watch the news, read the newspaper, or observe what is happening in the lives of people around you.

In preparation for storywriting, spend several minutes brainstorming with the help of a friend, teacher, or family member to gather ideas of situations and conflicts. Write down all the situations and possible resulting conflicts that come to mind. Then choose the one conflict that most interests you for your imaginative story.

Tone Your attitude toward the conflict will create the **tone** of your story. The details and language that you use might evoke joy, fear, amusement, grief, or some other emotion. For example, you will want your story to make the reader laugh if you feel that the situation facing the characters is funny. On the other hand, if you feel that the situation is serious and worrisome, you will try to increase the reader's anxiety.

After choosing your conflict, plan how you will establish the tone of your story by answering the following questions:

1. What is my attitude toward the conflict and the characters involved in it?

2. What details can I use to create this mood, or evoke these emotions, in the reader?

Point of View You may tell your story from either the first-person or third-person point of view.

In the first-person point of view, the story is narrated, using the pronoun *I*, by one person who either participates in or witnesses the conflict. Only the narrator's thoughts are expressed, as in the example below.

> *Charles stuffed a mysterious envelope into my hand and left without an explanation.*

In the third-person, or omniscient, point of view, the story is narrated by someone outside the story, someone who knows everything—each character's thoughts and actions. This allows the writer to reveal what any character thinks or does, as in the example that follows.

Somewhat embarrassed, Charles just stuffed the Valentine into Margaret's hand and walked away without a word.

Before you begin writing your imaginative story, you must choose an appropriate point of view from which to tell about the conflict.

Characters To create a captivating story, you must develop interesting and believable characters. Engaged in a struggle, the main character, or *protagonist*, might be opposed by another character, an *antagonist*. There may be other characters as well.

As you develop your characters, attempt to keep them consistent in their behavior and show logical reasons for any change in their behavior. For example, if an ordinarily greedy character suddenly acts generously, you must explain why.

Invent your characters by noting their physical appearances, actions, and personality traits.

Dialogue Dialogue is the spoken words of characters. A character's words can reveal things about the character's personality, background, thoughts, and attitudes. You can use dialogue to develop your characters and make your story more interesting.

Spend a few minutes brainstorming in order to gather ideas about your main characters. Give each one a name, some physical attributes, and a distinctive personality.

Setting The setting is the time and place of the action. Vivid, specific details help to describe the setting of a story. You must consider both location and time. Does your story take place indoors, in a specific room; or outdoors, on a mountain, beach, or prairie? Or, does it take place on an airplane, boat, or train? Do the events occur in the morning, afternoon, or evening? Does the story happen in the past, present, or future?

Decide where and when your story will take place and jot down a few details that you can use later to describe your setting.

Plot The plot is the action of your story. Once you have chosen a conflict, one or more characters, and the setting of your story, you are ready to develop the action using this story plan:

> BEGINNING OF STORY
>
> > Present your characters.
> >
> > Establish the setting and tone.
> >
> > Introduce the conflict.
>
> MIDDLE OF STORY
>
> > List a series of actions that build to a climax.
>
> END OF STORY
>
> > Resolve the conflict or show why it cannot be resolved.

Use the plan above to make notes, which you can expand later into a full imaginative story.

Practice Follow the instructions in this lesson for brainstorming, choosing a conflict, deciding on the tone and point of view, inventing characters, describing the setting, and planning the plot of your imaginative story. On a separate piece of paper, answer the following questions:

1. Who are your characters? Give a brief description of each.

2. What is the setting? Give the time and place.

3. Describe the tone or the emotions the reader will experience.

4. What is the conflict?

5. Briefly list some actions that will build to a climax.

6. How will you resolve the conflict?

Keep your answers to these questions in your three-ring binder. In the next lesson, you will use this information as you write your imaginative story.

LESSON 29

Writing an Imaginative Story

In Lesson 28, you prepared to write your imaginative story. By brainstorming, you gathered ideas and details. You chose a conflict, decided on the tone and point of view, invented characters, described your setting, and roughly planned the plot. Now you are ready to write the imaginative story.

Keep this plan in front of you as you write:

BEGINNING OF STORY

    Present your characters.

    Establish the setting and tone.

    Introduce the conflict.

MIDDLE OF STORY

    List a series of actions that build to a climax.

END OF STORY

    Resolve the conflict or show why it cannot be resolved.

Practice Using your notes from Lesson 28 and the plan above, follow the steps below to write your story.

1. Write an introductory sentence ("hook") that will grab the reader's attention.

2. At the beginning of the story, in whatever order you think is best, establish the setting and tone, present your characters, and introduce the conflict.

3. Add dialogue in order to reveal more about your characters' personalities, thoughts, and motivations.

4. Keep the point of view consistent throughout the story.

5. Write a series of actions that build to a climax.

6. Resolve the conflict at the end of your story or show why it cannot be resolved.

LESSON 30

Evaluating the Imaginative Story

Because *writing is a process* and all of our writing is "work in progress," we constantly make changes to improve our work. This is especially true when writing an imaginative story. As you create your story, you may see opportunities for revisiting previous parts of your story in order to add more or different traits to a character to explain his or her actions.

Evaluating Your Writing

In Lesson 29, you completed your imaginative story. Now that some time has passed, you are ready to evaluate it using the following guidelines.

Ask yourself these questions:

- Does my introductory sentence ("hook") capture the reader's attention?

- Does the beginning of the story establish the tone and suggest the conflict?

- Are the characters believable and interesting?

- Have I revealed the characters' personalities and motivations through dialogue and action as well as description?

- Are my characters consistent in their behavior? Have I adequately explained any changes from their normal behavior?

- Are there other details, modifiers, comparisons, or sensory expressions I could add to help the reader to visualize the setting?

- Do the actions flow logically from one to another?

- Do the actions build suspense?

- Does the dialogue sound natural?

- Does the point of view remain constant throughout the story?

- Are some of my sentences weak or confusing? Should any be removed because they do not relate to the story?

- Do my sentences appear in the best possible order? Could I place them in a different order that is more logical or effective?

- Is each sentence constructed as well as it should be? *Read each sentence in each paragraph as if it were the only sentence on the page. This helps you to catch sentence fragments, run-on sentences, misspellings, and grammatical errors.*

- Is the end of the story believable and satisfying? Has the conflict been resolved, or have I shown that it cannot be resolved?

Practice Use the Evaluation Form on the following page to evaluate the imaginative story you wrote for Lesson 29. Read your story carefully as you check for the items listed on the Evaluation Form. Write YES or NO in the blank next to each question.

When you are finished, either you will be confident that you have a strong imaginative story, or you will know where it needs to be improved.

If you answered NO to one or more of the questions on the Evaluation Form, rewrite to improve those areas.

When you can answer YES to every question on the Evaluation Form, you will have completed this assignment.

Imaginative Story Evaluation Form

Title: _____

_____ Does my introductory sentence ("hook") capture the reader's attention?

_____ Does the beginning of the story establish the tone and suggest the conflict?

_____ Are the characters believable and interesting?

_____ Have I revealed the characters' personalities and motivations through dialogue and action as well as description?

_____ Are my characters consistent in their behavior? Have I adequately explained any change from their normal behavior?

_____ Have I included sufficient details, modifiers, comparisons, and sensory expressions to enable the reader to visualize the setting?

_____ Do the actions flow logically from one to another?

_____ Do the actions build suspense?

_____ Does the dialogue sound natural?

_____ Does the point of view remain consistent throughout the story?

_____ Is each sentence strong and clear? Does each sentence relate to the story?

_____ Is each sentence structured as well as it could be? *Read each sentence in each paragraph as if it were the only sentence on the page. This helps you identify sentence fragments, run-on sentences, and the overall strength or weakness of each sentence.*

_____ Is the end of the story believable and satisfying? Has the conflict been resolved, or have I shown that the conflict cannot be resolved?

Writing a Short Story Summary

We have learned that a summary condenses a longer passage to a shorter one, leaving out details and giving only the main ideas of the original passage. In this lesson, we shall practice writing a one-paragraph summary of a short story.

Short Story Summary
If you had read an interesting short story and wanted to tell a friend about it, you might give your friend a *summary* of the story. You would not tell the *whole* story or give away the ending. Instead, you would summarize, giving some general information about the main characters, setting, and major conflict.

Example
Below is a summary of the short story, "The Tidy Drawer," by Mo McAuley. Notice that we use the present tense of verbs.

> Abby's bedroom is really messy. Her mother suggests she clean it to earn some pocket change. Soon the clutter disappears from Abby's room, and she begins rummaging through the "tidy drawer" with her mother to find the coin purse. They might not come across the coin purse, but the tidy drawer contains treasures that make for many laughs.
>
> Summary by Lizzy Workmore

Practice
Write a one-paragraph summary of the imaginative story that you wrote for Lesson 29. Your paragraph should not exceed eight sentences. Your summary should include general information about main characters, setting, and plot. Use the present tense of verbs.

Additional Practice
Read one of the short stories suggested below or one that your teacher suggests. Then put the book away and write a one-paragraph summary of the story. Your paragraph should not exceed eight sentences. Your summary should include general information about main characters, setting, and plot.

Suggested reading:

"The Red Shoes," by Hans Christian Anderson

"Marmalade," by Sonja Cheal

"The Hare Who Would Not Be King," by Tish Farrell

"Rapunzel," by Brothers Grimm

"Rip Van Winkle," by Washington Irving

"The Selfish Giant," by Oscar Wilde

Writing in Response to Literature

You read books and magazines for pleasure; however, there are times when you are expected to analyze and reflect on what you read. This is called active reading. In active reading, you ask yourself what kind of text are you reading. Is the text fictional? an essay? an editorial?

Then you decide on the author's purpose. Is it to entertain, to inform, or to persuade? Next you pinpoint the main idea or find the thesis. Finally you find evidence to support your thoughts on the main idea or thesis.

*Special Note: You will use complete sentences and the present tense of verbs when you are answering questions about the text.

In this lesson, we will read an excerpt from *Black Beauty* by Anna Sewell and practice writing in response to it.

> The wind was then much higher, and I heard the master say to John, he had never been out in such a storm....
>
> [Suddenly] there was a groan and a crack, and a splitting sound, and tearing, crashing down among the other trees came an oak, torn up by the roots, and it fell right across the road just before us. I will never say I was not frightened, for I was. I stopped still, and I believe I trembled....John jumped out and was in a moment in my head.
>
> "That was a very near touch," said my master. "What's to be done now?"
>
> "Well, sir, we can't drive over that tree nor yet get round it; there will be nothing for it, but to go back to the four crossways, and . . . round to the wooden bridge...."
>
> So back we went and round by the crossroads; but by the time we got to the bridge, it was very nearly dark. We could just see that the water was over the middle of it; but as that happened sometimes when the floods were out, master did not stop. We were going

along at a good pace, but the moment my feet touched the first part of the bridge I felt sure there was something wrong. I dared not go forward, and I made a dead stop. "Go on, Beauty," said my master, and he gave me a touch of the whip, but I dared not stir; he gave a sharp cut, I jumped, but I dared not go forward.

"There's something wrong, sir," said John, and he sprang out of the dogcart and came to my head and looked all about. He tried to lead me forward. "Come on, Beauty, what's the matter?" Of course I could not tell him, but I knew very well that the bridge was not safe.

Just then the man at the tollgate on the other side rode out of the house, tossing a torch like mad.

"Hoy, hoy, hoy, halloo, stop!" he cried.

"What's the matter?" shouted my master.

"The bridge is broken in the middle, and part of it is carried away; if you come on you'll be in the river."

"Thank God!" said my master. "You Beauty!" said John, and took the bridle and gently turned me round to the right-hand road by the riverside. The sun had set some time, the wind seemed to have lulled off after the furious blast which tore up the tree. It grew darker and darker, stiller and stiller. I trotted quietly along, the wheels hardly making a sound on the soft road.

Practice Refer to the selection and answer the following questions. You may work alone, with your teacher, or with other students. Remember to use the present tense of verbs in your answers.

1. Why does the author write this selection?

2. What is the effect of beginning the selection with a storm?

3. To which sense do the descriptions in the second paragraph appeal?

4. What is the theme of this selection?

5. How might the master's experience help him the next time he is caught in a storm with Beauty?

Writing in Response to Informational Text

Sometimes you read books and magazines to learn something new or to learn more about a subject. There are times when you are expected to practice active reading: to analyze and reflect on what you read.

In this lesson, we shall read for information. Carefully read the nonfiction selection.

> Halley's Comet is expected to be visible again in the United States in the year 2062. The comet passes within sight of Earth only once about every 76 years, so most people only get to see it once in their lifetime.

> Edmund Halley was an English astronomer who first saw the comet in 1682. It lit up the night sky for weeks, and many people feared that it would never disappear. People were afraid that the comet would come down on Earth and cause the death of many people. Halley tried to tell the public that they had nothing to fear from the comet. He based his belief on his friend Isaac Newton's fairly new scientific theories on gravity. Using these theories, Halley predicted that the comet would return again in the year 1758.

> As Halley predicted, the comet returned in 1758. It was Christmas night of that year. Halley died in 1742, so he couldn't verify the accuracy of his prediction. Because Halley was the person who had correctly predicted the comet's return, people started calling it "Halley's Comet."

> The comet came to be called "The Flaming Sword" because of its shape and the many stories about its sighting. Some people started to blame the comet for famine, war, and disease. They thought it was an evil star and an omen of bad events.

Practice After reading the selection, answer the following questions. You may work alone or with your teacher or with other students. Remember to use present tense when writing about literary texts.

1. According to the selection, how were Newton and Halley alike?

2. What does the word *verify* mean in this selection?

3. Why was the comet named after Edmund Halley?

4. What is the main idea of the selection?

*When you have completed the practice questions above, compare your answers to those in the Teacher Guide.

LESSON 34

Preparing to Write a Research Paper: The Working Bibliography

A research paper is a type of expository writing based on information gathered from a variety of reliable sources. In the future, you may be asked to write a research paper for an English, history, science, art, or music class. Knowing the procedure for writing a good research paper will help you to become a successful high school and college student.

In this lesson, you shall learn how to prepare for writing a research paper on an assigned subject. To practice the procedure, you may choose one of the following subjects:

1. The Bumblebee, a Necessary Insect

2. How the Automobile Began

3. Benjamin Franklin's Contribution to the Development of Bifocals

4. How to Avoid Poison Oak in the Mountains

5. A subject suggested by your teacher

Tone The research paper requires a serious tone. The writing should be formal and impersonal. Therefore, we do not use first person pronouns, such as *I, me,* or *my.*

Gathering Sources of Information The first step in researching your subject is to compile a **working bibliography,** a collection of possible sources of information. Consider the following possibilities for your research:

• library research aids including card catalog, *Readers' Guide*, and reference works

• Internet

• government publications

• personal interviews or correspondence

• museums

• scholarly journals

Evaluating Sources of Information

Not all sources are reliable or useful. We must evaluate each source for its usefulness. Asking the following questions will help us to evaluate each source:

1. *Is the information current?* A 1970 study of the nation's economy is out-of-date. Therefore, it would not be an appropriate source for a paper on today's economy except for drawing comparisons with the past.

2. *Is the source objective and impartial?* An article written by the president of Molly's Dairy Products about the human body's requirement for dairy nutrients might not be an objective source. The author could be trying to sell you something.

3. *For what audience was the source intended?* Material written for young children might be over-simplified, and material written for specialists might be too technical.

Preparing Bibliography Cards

After gathering sources, evaluating each one for its usefulness, and choosing only those that are appropriate, we are ready to compile a working bibliography, the list of sources from which we will glean information for our research paper.

Using three-inch by five-inch index cards, we record each source on a separate card. We include all the information that follows, for we will need it to prepare our final bibliography when our paper is completed.

BOOKS

1. Author's (or editor's) full name, last name first. Indicate editor by placing *ed.* after the name. If the book has more than one author, only the first author is written last name first. Others are written first name first.

2. Title and subtitle underlined

3. City of publication

4. Publisher's name

5. Most recent copyright year

MAGAZINE, NEWSPAPER, JOURNAL, AND ENCYCLOPEDIA ARTICLES

1. Author's (or editor's) full name, last name first. Indicate editor by placing *ed.* after the name. If the article has more than one author, only the first author is written last name first. Others are written first name first.

2. Title of article in quotation marks

3. Name of magazine, newspaper, journal, or encyclopedia underlined

4. Date and page numbers of magazines
   Date, edition, section, page numbers of newspapers
   Volume, year, page numbers of journals
   Edition and year of encyclopedias

ELECTRONIC SOURCES

1. Author's (or editor's) full name, last name first. Indicate editor by placing *ed.* after the name. If the article has more than one author, only the first author is written last name first. Others are written first name first.

2. Title of article in quotation marks

3. Books, magazines, newspapers, journals, encyclopedias, or Web sites underlined

4. Date and page numbers of magazines

   Date, edition, section, page numbers of newspapers

   Volume, year, page numbers of journals

   Edition and year of encyclopedias

   City of publication, publisher's name, and most recent copyright year of books

5. The date that you accessed the source

6. The URL in angle brackets

We assign each bibliography card a "source number" and write it in the upper left corner. Later, we will use this number to identify the sources of our notes. Below are some sample bibliography cards.

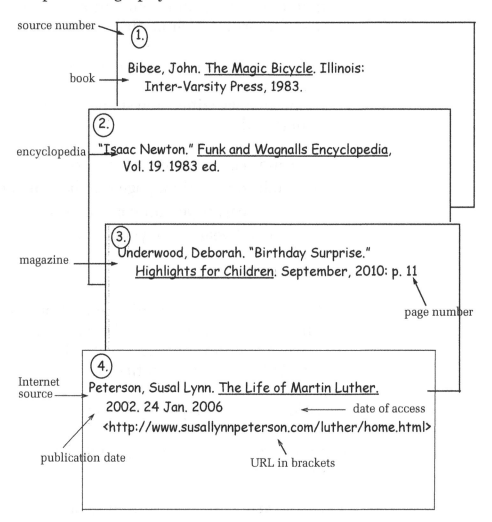

source number

① 1.

book → Bibee, John. The Magic Bicycle. Illinois:
        Inter-Varsity Press, 1983.

② 2.

encyclopedia "Isaac Newton." Funk and Wagnalls Encyclopedia,
              Vol. 19. 1983 ed.

③ 3.

magazine → Underwood, Deborah. "Birthday Surprise."
            Highlights for Children. September, 2010: p. 11

page number

④ 4.

Internet source → Peterson, Susal Lynn. The Life of Martin Luther.
                   2002. 24 Jan. 2006   ← date of access
                   <http://www.susallynnpeterson.com/luther/home.html>

publication date   URL in brackets

Practice After you have chosen a subject from the list of suggestions for your research paper, follow the instructions in this lesson for gathering and evaluating sources and for preparing bibliography cards. Locate at least four appropriate sources and prepare a bibliography card for each one. Remember to assign each card a source number and write it in the upper left corner.

Preparing to Write a Research Paper: Notes, Thesis, Outline

In the last lesson, you chose a subject for a research paper and created a working bibliography. This listed at least four sources of information that you will use for your paper. In this lesson, you will take notes from these sources, organize your notes, create a thesis statement, and develop an outline for your paper.

Taking Notes It is helpful to use four-inch by six-inch index cards for taking notes. As you read through your sources, write down information that applies to your subject. Write most of your notes in your own words. You may summarize the author's main ideas, or you may record specific facts or details in your own words. If you quote the author, you must enclose the author's exact words in quotation marks.

Whenever you take notes from a source, you must credit that source whether you quote an author or use your own words. Do not *plagiarize*, or use another person's words or ideas without acknowledging the source.

In the upper right corner of your note card, you will enter the source number from your working bibliography.

At the end of each note, write the page or pages on which you found the information.

Below is a sample note card.

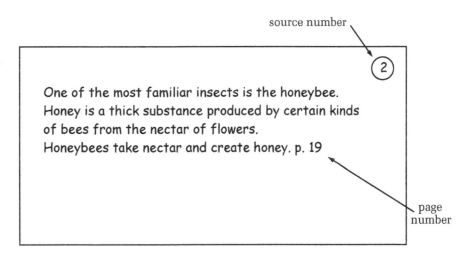

Organizing Your Information After you have taken notes on all your sources and gathered sufficient information for your research paper, take some time to organize your note cards and arrange them in a logical order.

Thesis Statement Now look over your organized notes and write a thesis statement that clearly explains the main idea of your research paper.

Outline In Lesson 17, you learned to develop an outline. Use your organized note cards to help you create an informal topic outline for your research paper. This outline will guide you as you begin to write the first draft of your paper in the next lesson.

Practice Follow the instructions in this lesson for taking notes from your sources. Then organize your notes, write a thesis statement, and develop an outline for your research paper.

Writing the Research Paper

In the last lesson, you took notes from your sources, organized your notes, wrote a thesis statement, and created an outline for your research paper.

Writing the First Draft With your outline, your thesis statement, your notes, and your bibliography cards in front of you, you are ready to begin writing the first draft of your research paper. A first draft is a rough copy that is for your use only. It is meant to be revised again and again until you are satisfied with it.

As you write, keep in mind your thesis statement, your purpose, and the need for a formal tone. Use the information on your note cards to support your thesis and to fill in the details as you follow your outline for organization.

Create an opening paragraph that captures the reader's attention. Consider beginning with an interesting statement, an anecdote, or an example. Make certain that your opening paragraph includes your thesis statement.

Use the main points in your outline to create topic sentences for your body paragraphs. Then expand these topic sentences into paragraphs, making sure that all of your information relates to your thesis statement.

Pay special attention to transitions as you begin each new paragraph.

Your concluding paragraph will summarize and reinforce the ideas set forth in the rest of your research paper.

Documentation of Sources Writing the first draft of a research paper involves bringing together information from your different sources, which you must acknowledge properly. We call this **documentation of sources.**

As you write, you must credit your sources for both ideas and quotations. There are various methods of documenting sources for research papers. In this book, we shall practice a method called *parenthetical citations.* This form identifies sources in parentheses that are placed as close as possible to the ideas or quotations that we cite.

Inside the parentheses, we place a reference to the source on our bibliography card. Usually, the reference inside the parentheses consists only of an author's last name and page number from which the material was taken.

For example, (Smith 31) would appear right after an idea taken from page thirty-one in Albert Smith's book.

When no author and only a title is given for a source, we place a shortened form of the title and the page number or numbers in the parentheses: ("Fly in the Ointment" 110-111).

In the example below, notice that the end punctuation for a sentence containing borrowed material is placed *after* the parenthetical citation.

> Charles Dickens invented clever nicknames such as "the artful dodger" (Smith 31). ⟵ punctuation mark

The highly respected Modern Language Association (MLA) gives us many more detailed guidelines for parenthetical citations. However, in this lesson, we shall follow the simplified instructions provided.

The Bibliography

The **bibliography,** the list of the sources that you used as you wrote your paper, comes at the end of the research paper.

Follow these steps to create your bibliography:

1. Alphabetize your bibliography cards according to the last names of the authors or the first important word in a title if there is no author.

2. Copy the information from all of your alphabetized bibliography cards under the title "Bibliography" or "Works Cited."

3. Indent all lines after the first line of each entry and punctuate as shown in the example below.

Bibliography

Kramer, Pamela. "Share Tactics." Family Circle,
    October, 2009: 74-79.

Leach, Daniel. Helpful Insects. New York, Grassvale
    Publishers, 2007.

In high school and college, you will learn to follow more detailed guidelines for bibliographic entries. However, in this lesson you may follow the simplified instructions provided unless your teacher advises you to do otherwise.

<u>Practice</u> Follow the procedure given in this lesson for writing the first draft of your research paper and for creating your bibliography, or list of works cited.

LESSON 37

Evaluating the Research Paper

The knowledge that *writing is a process* guides our thinking throughout the construction of our research paper. From the first steps in choosing our subject, to gathering information and organizing our thoughts, to creating body paragraphs, to adding transitions, we constantly make changes to improve our work.

Evaluating Your Writing

In the last lesson, you completed the first draft of your research paper. Now that some time has passed, you are ready to evaluate it using the following guidelines.

Ask yourself these questions:

- Are my sources reliable, objective, and current?

- Is my introductory sentence interesting? *If it is not interesting to you, it certainly will not be interesting to the reader.*

- Does my thesis clearly state the purpose of my paper?

- Does the beginning of the research paper clearly establish a formal, serious tone?

- Does each body paragraph have a clear topic sentence at the beginning that tells the reader exactly what the paragraph will be about? *Read each topic sentence without the rest of the paragraph to see if it can stand alone as a strong idea.*

- Does each paragraph include specific details and examples from my research?

- Have I correctly documented each piece of borrowed information?

- Are my sentences in a logical order?

- Does each paragraph (except for the first) begin with an effective transition?

- Are there other details that I can add as additional body paragraphs to create a fuller or more complete paper?

- Are some of my sentences weak or confusing? Should they be removed because they do not relate to my thesis?

- Do my body paragraphs appear in the best possible order? Could I place them in a different order that is more logical or effective?

- Is each sentence constructed as well as it should be? *Read each sentence in each paragraph as if it were the only sentence on the page. This helps you to catch sentence fragments, run-on sentences, misspellings, and grammatical errors.*

- Does my ending paragraph obviously conclude my presentation? Does it reinforce my thesis statement?

Practice Use the Evaluation Form on the following page to evaluate the research paper you wrote for Lesson 36. Read your research paper carefully as you check for the items listed on the Evaluation Form. Write YES or NO in the blank next to each question.

When you are finished, either you will be confident that you have a strong research paper, or you will know where it needs to be improved.

If you answered NO to one or more of the questions on the Evaluation Form, rewrite to improve those areas.

When you can answer YES to every question on the Evaluation Form, you will have completed this assignment.

Research Paper Evaluation Form

Subject: _____

_____ Is my introductory sentence interesting? *If it is not interesting to you, it certainly will not be interesting to the reader.*

_____ Does the beginning of the research paper clearly establish a formal, serious tone?

_____ Does the thesis clearly state the purpose of the paper?

_____ Does each body paragraph have a clear topic sentence at the beginning that tells the reader exactly what the paragraph will be about? *Read each topic sentence without the rest of the paragraph to see if it can stand alone as a strong idea.*

_____ Do the details all contribute to the reader's understanding of the thesis?

_____ Within each paragraph, are my sentences in a logical or practical order?

_____ Does each paragraph (except for the first paragraph) begin with an effective transition?

_____ Is each piece of borrowed material given proper credit?

_____ Are all of my sentences strong and clear? Do they all directly relate to the thesis?

_____ Do my body paragraphs appear in the best possible order? Is their order logical and effective?

_____ Is each sentence structured as well as it could be? *Read each sentence in each paragraph as if it were the only sentence on the page. This helps you identify sentence fragments, run-on sentences, and the overall strength or weakness of each sentence.*

_____ Does my concluding paragraph summarize my research and reinforce my thesis statement?

_____ Are my sources reliable, objective, and current?

Idioms and Proverbs

Idioms   An **idiom** is a phrase or expression whose meaning cannot be understood from the dictionary meanings of the words in it. For example, "Hold your tongue" is an English idiom meaning "be quiet" or "keep still."

Practice   Working by yourself or with others, write the meaning of each English idiom below.

1. lose your marbles

   _____

2. new kid on the block

   _____

3. give your two cents

   _____

4. keep in stitches

   _____

5. stumble into

   _____

6. in a rut

   _____

Can you think of other English idioms? List as many as you can and write their meanings.

Proverbs   A **proverb,** or adage, is a short, wise saying used for a long time by many people. "Don't put the cart before the horse" is a proverb meaning "do not reverse the normal order of things."

Practice   Working by yourself or with others, write the meanings of the proverbs below.

1. Birds of a feather flock together.

   _____

2. A leopard cannot change its spots.

   _____

3. A stitch in time saves nine.

   _____

4. All that glitters is not gold.

   _____

5. Beauty is only skin deep.

   _____

6. Every cloud has a silver lining.

   _____

Can you think of other proverbs? List as many as you can and write their meanings.

*When you have finished this lesson, compare your answers to those in the Teacher Guide.

Circle the simple subject and underline the simple predicate in each sentence.

1. The Earth turns.

2. The Sun shines all the time.

3. We see it during the daytime.

4. Does the Sun sleep at night?

5. Can animals live without sunlight?

6. Can plants live without sunlight?

7. We need the Sun's light and warmth.

8. Dark clouds were covering the city.

9. The Sun had disappeared.

10. Down came the rain.

11. Thunder rumbled in the distance.

12. Fido splashed through the puddles.

13. Do you have an umbrella?

14. The rain has stopped.

15. Out came the Sun.

16. My tomato plants are growing!

17. The seeds have sprouted.

18. Have you planted a garden?

19. Soon we shall pick some zucchini.

20. Does Fido like zucchini?

Circle each letter that should be capitalized in the sentences below.

1. my friend kelly crossed the famous golden gate bridge in san francisco, california.

2. the panama canal connects the pacific ocean and the caribbean sea.

3. the amazon river in south america flows into the atlantic ocean.

4. i think niagara falls, between lake erie and lake ontario, is spectacular!

5. you will find the andes mountains in south america.

6. in the center of canada lies lake winnipeg.

7. phil hopes to sing the famous hymn "amazing grace" at carnegie hall in new york city next april.

8. last wednesday, i read the poem "trees" by joyce kilmer.

9. mr. gallup teaches at pasadena city college in california.

10. is concord the capital of new hampshire?

11. have you ever swum in the mediterranean sea?

12. monty and allison surf in the pacific ocean.

13. yes, boston is the capital of massachusetts.

14. the *titanic*, a luxury ship from great britain, hit an iceberg off the coast of newfoundland.

15. last july the rivas family camped near the grand canyon in arizona.

Circle each helping verb in the following sentences.

1. Long ago, Alabama was called the Cotton State.

2. People may see moose, elk, caribou, and bears in Alaska.

3. Someday I shall visit the Grand Canyon in Arizona.

4. We might search for diamonds in Arkansas!

5. Gold was found in California in 1848.

6. Next winter Brent will be skiing in Colorado.

7. The Connecticut Colony had written a constitution more than a hundred years before the War of Independence.

8. Do people still live in Delaware's colonial homes?

9. In Florida's Everglades, a crocodile is sleeping peacefully.

10. Former President Jimmy Carter was born in Georgia.

11. Did this pineapple come from Hawaii?

12. Do all potatoes come from Idaho?

13. Our plane will land at O'Hare Airport in Chicago, Illinois, at 7:30 p.m.

14. Does Indiana manufacture baseball bats?

15. Nathan has been packing popcorn in Iowa for thirty years.

16. Have you driven through the wheat fields of Kansas?

17. Buffalo were wandering through the Kentucky mountains.

18. The Mississippi Delta has provided rich farmland in Louisiana.

19. People in Maine have built many ships.

20. Did your ship sail into the Chesapeake Bay in Maryland?

Corny Chronicle #1
Follows Lesson 13

The Fundraiser

Three clever friends, (1) _____, (2) _____,

proper noun (person)   proper noun (person)

and (3) _____, wanted to raise money to purchase
proper noun (person)

more (4) _____ for (5) _____. Their plan was to
concrete plural noun   proper noun (place)

manufacture (6) _____ from (7) _____ and sell
concrete plural noun   concrete plural noun

them to (8) _____, (9) _____, and others who
proper noun (person)   proper noun (person)

might be interested.

In preparation for the project, the three clever friends

(10) _____ and (11) _____ for many hours.
past tense action verb   past tense action verb

United in their efforts, they were truly a (12) _____.
collective noun

After working together for nearly (13) _____
number

weeks, they finally had their first product to sell. It looked

like a (14) _____ but made them think of
concrete singular noun

(15) _____ or (16) _____. Thrilled with their
abstract singular noun   abstract singular noun

product, they felt sure that either (17) _____ or
proper noun (person)

(18) _____ would buy it from them although
proper noun (person)

(19) _____ doubted that it would sell.
proper noun (person)

In the end the three clever friends were able to sell their

magnificent product for (20) _____ dollars to
number

(21) _____, who plans to rent a storage compartment
proper noun (person)

for it in (22) _____.
proper noun (place)

Teacher instructions:

(1) Have students number blank, lined papers from 1 to 22. Ask them to write an example of the part of speech indicated beside each number. Proceed slowly, making sure students have written correct examples.

(2) Give each student a copy of the story. Ask students to write each word from their list into the blank with the corresponding number.

(3) Ask some students to read their stories aloud.

Circle each letter that should be capitalized in the following sentences, poems, and song lyrics (capitalized like poems).

1. stephen foster wrote some humorous songs during the 1800s. my friends and i like to sing them around the campfire.

2. i come from alabama

wid my banjo on my knee,

i'm gwan to louisiana

my true love for to see,

it rained all night the day i left,

the weather it was dry,

the sun so hot i froze to death,

susanna, don't you cry.

—stephen foster

3. my teacher said that i should stop giggling, but i couldn't stop because i was reading poems by ogden nash. they were so funny!

4. a dog that is indoors

to be let out implores.

you let him out and what then?

he wants back in again.

—ogden nash

5. the ant has made himself illustrious

through constant industry industrous.

so what?

would you be calm and placid

if you were full of acid?

—ogden nash

6. now another day is breaking,

sleep was sweet and so is waking.

dear Lord, i promised you last night

never again to sulk or fight.

such vows are easier to keep

when a child is sound asleep.

—ogden nash

Circle each letter that should be capitalized in the following titles.

1. "down in the valley"

2. "a bicycle built for two"

3. "in the good old summertime"

4. "the man on the flying trapeze"

5. "the stars and stripes forever"

6. *the indian in the cupboard*

7. *the house at pooh corner*

8. *the voyages of dr. doolittle*

9. *the lion, the witch, and the wardrobe*

10. *the only game in town*

11. *where the red fern grows*

12. *the wind in the willows*

13. *old yeller*

14. *the phantom tollbooth*

15. *the sign of the beaver*

16. *emil and the detectives*

17. *the trumpet of the swan*

18. *the mouse and the motorcycle*

19. *my side of the mountain*

20. *little house on the prairie*

Circle each letter that should be capitalized in the following sentences and outlines.

1. confucius said, "virtue is not left to stand alone. he who practices it will have neighbors."

2. have you read *alice's adventures in wonderland* by lewis carroll?

3. yesterday i read a story called "aladdin and the wonderful lamp."

4. tonight i shall read "ali baba and the forty thieves."

5. as anabel drove toward boston, she sang her favorite song, "my old kentucky home."

6. I. the orchestra
   A. percussion and strings
   B. the brass family
   C. the woodwind family

7. II. types of musical compositions
   A. the waltz
   B. the march
   C. the symphony

8. benjamin franklin said, "one today is worth two tomorrows."

9. he also said, "a lie stands on one leg, truth on two."

10. "the ballad of the boll weevil" is an american folk song.

11. in 1892, john muir, an american naturalist, wrote to the editor of a magazine, "let us do something to make the mountains glad."

12. john muir wrote about the beauty of nature in a book called *the mountains of california.*

13. pearl s. buck's most popular novel, *the good earth*, won the pulitzer prize.

14. james thurber, an american humorist, wrote a story called "the secret life of walter mitty."

Circle each letter that should be capitalized in the following sentences.

1. if grandpa zamora grew up in nicaragua, why doesn't he speak english with an accent?

2. Yes, captain cheung met ms. phan aboard the ship to india.

3. next year i shall take classes such as spanish, art, geography, mathematics, and english.

4. although dr. adan has taught history, he has never taught american government.

5. before aunt catherine traveled to japan, she studied japanese.

6. yes, i believe mom and dad invited mr. and mrs. fernando cabrera to their anniversary party in june.

7. while in europe, mom took classes in art history and french.

8. yesterday sergeant mundy told miss lu that he could do nothing about the flock of canadian geese in her yard.

9. during our two-hour social studies class, i noticed that even the teacher, dr. dreamer, was yawning.

10. i promised mother that i would clean the garage on saturday.

11. i assured father that i would find a safe place to store his fishing pole.

12. when aunt tanisha took chemistry, there were fewer than a hundred known elements.

13. does deputy cruz always comb her hair like that?

14. no, uncle wassim, i cannot go fishing, for i have to do a homework assignment for language arts.

Corny Chronicle #2
Follows Lesson 39

The Parade

(1) _____ and (2) _____ are organizing a
<u>proper noun (person)</u>   <u>proper noun (person)</u>

parade to honor their (3) _____. Floats decorated with
<u>collective noun</u>

(4) _____ and (5) _____ to portray the parade's
<u>concrete plural noun</u>   <u>concrete plural noun</u>

theme of (6) _____ will follow (7) _____, the
<u>abstract singular noun</u>   <u>proper noun (person)</u>

grand marshall, through the streets of the city.

Teacher instructions:

(1) Have students number blank, lined papers from 1 to 26. Ask them to write an example of the part of speech indicated beside each number. Proceed slowly, making sure students have written correct examples.

(2) Give each student a copy of the story. Ask students to write each word from their list into the blank with the corresponding number.

(3) Ask some students to read their stories aloud.

People from (8) _____ and as far away as
<u>proper noun (place)</u>

(9) _____ will gather to watch the parade. They will
<u>proper noun (place)</u>

see horses (10) _____ (11) _____ and
<u>present participle form of action verb</u>   <u>preposition</u>

(12) _____ the street. Balloons will fly
<u>preposition</u>

(13) _____ and (14) _____ the spectators as
<u>preposition</u>   <u>preposition</u>

marching bands (15) _____, (16) _____, and
<u>present tense action verb</u>   <u>present tense action verb</u>

(17) _____ to the beat of (18) _____ drums and
<u>present tense action verb</u>   <u>descriptive adjective</u>

the clash of (19) _____ cymbals.
<u>descriptive adjective</u>

The most (20) _____ part of the parade will be
<u>descriptive adjective</u>

(21) _____ bicycle (22) _____, which will
<u>proper possessive noun (person)</u>   <u>collective noun</u>

feature (23) _____ cyclists (24) _____
<u>adjective (number)</u>   <u>present participle form of action verb</u>

(25) _____ banners advertising (26) _____.
<u>preposition</u>   <u>abstract noun</u>

Limiting adjectives include the following:

    Articles (*a, an, the*)

    Demonstrative adjectives (*this, that, these, those*)

    Numbers (*one, two, three*, etc.)

    Possessive adjectives (*my, his, her, Bob's, Meg's*, etc.)

    Indefinites (*some, many, few*, etc.)

Circle each limiting adjective that you find in the following sentences.

1. Delaware's capital is Dover.

2. In the north, Delaware's width narrows to ten miles.

3. Jeff's aunt works at a shipyard in that state.

4. Her son left his gloves in my car.

5. Many people live in the city of Wilmington.

6. Delaware has much industry.

7. From the shore I could see several ships in the bay.

8. Have those sailors lost their way?

9. This state wants to protect its beaches from pollution.

10. Have you seen any gulls in your area?

Complete the following sentence diagrams.

1. Maine's mills produce much paper.

2. That business makes many computer components.

3. Maine has a cool, moist climate.

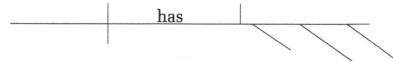

4. Two chickadees eat some seeds.

Circle each letter that should be capitalized in the following sentences.

1. my grandfather worked in a kentucky coal mine for forty years.

2. every fall i play football with my cousins.

3. uncle thurgood wants to tour an alabama auto assembly plant.

4. the louisiana cotton fields stretch as far as i can see.

5. last summer i helped grandpa husk the iowa corn for our meal.

6. when georgia peaches ripen, aunt rosa will pick a bushel.

7. have you smelled the blossoms on florida orange trees?

8. my brother likes peanut butter, but my sister prefers wisconsin cheese.

9. a french chef served mother and me a plate of steaming california vegetables.

10. would you rather have boston baked beans or idaho potatoes tonight?

11. musicians on xylophones, tambourines, and african drums created rhythms to accompany the chorus.

12. during spring vacation we shall play afternoon baseball games and evening chinese checkers tournaments.

13. mario's grandfather played a steinway piano in the town's largest concert hall.

14. i think cousin foster's dog is a welsh terrier.

15. a calico cat rode the muscular german shepherd with a beagle named tux right behind.

16. uncle bob planted petunias and marigolds beneath his australian willow trees.

Add periods as needed in each sentence or outline below. Then circle each period.

1. I The state of Kansas

    A Industry

    B Agriculture

2. Herbert C Hoover was the thirty-first President of the United States

3. J Edgar Hoover, who served as director of the Federal Bureau of Investigation, worked hard to stop organized crime

4. Make the most of today

5. General Robert E Lee surrendered to General Ulysses S Grant on April 9, 1865, in Virginia

6. We shall read C S Lewis's *Chronicles of Narnia* before we see the movie

7. I The Southwest

    A Arizona

    B New Mexico

    C Oklahoma

    D Texas

8. Study the fifty states and their capitals

9. Isabel M Angles taught algebra at Francisco P Cruz High School

10. I The state of Michigan

    A History

    B Government

    C Economy

11. Officer U B Ware arrested Captain I M Loud for disturbing the peace

12. Please turn down the volume

Diagram the simple subject and simple predicate of each sentence.

1. Florida and California produce citrus fruits.

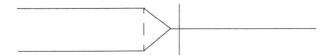

2. Mud-drenched frogs croak and leap around the pond.

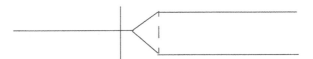

3. Elk, moose, and bison roam in Wyoming.

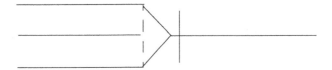

4. A coyote pauses and howls at the moon.

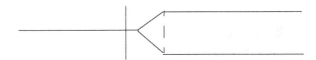

5. Maine, Vermont, and Massachusetts border New Hampshire.

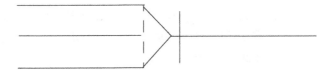

6. Amelia smiled and waved at Elle.

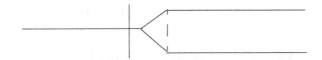

Add periods as needed. Circle each period.

1. Mr Yu took the 10:30 am bus to Farmer's Market on S Fifth Street

2. There he purchased bananas, grapes, potatoes, etc for his family

3. Altogether he spent $3042 (thirty dollars and forty-two cents) on misc (miscellaneous) fruits and vegetables

4. At 1:30 pm, he boarded the bus on W Spring Ave to ride home

5. Along the bus route, a sign read, "This road closed until Thurs, Feb 3"

6. Mr Yu's bus moved slowly through traffic on Mt Carmel Rd, a detour

7. Mrs Yu feared that her husband would be late for his 4:20 pm appointment with Dr Hatchet

8. However, Mr Yu reached the Hope Medical Bldg on the SE corner of York Pl just in time

9. "The gerontology dept has moved to the seventh floor," read a sign

10. Breathing hard from climbing stairs, Mr Yu paid his $6850 (sixty-eight dollars and fifty cents) to the receptionist

11. Then he sat down next to an Antz-Be-Gone, Inc, employee, who smelled like pesticide and reminded Mr Yu of an old acquaintance, Capt Cheesebreath

12. After waiting over an hour, Mr Yu heard the receptionist say that Dr Hatchet was performing an emergency appendectomy and would not see any more patients until 9:15 am the following day

Corny Chronicle #3

Follows Lesson 51

A Field Trip

Three friends, (1)_____, (2)_____, and
proper noun (person)   proper noun (person)

(3)_____, were in charge of planning the annual class
proper noun (person)

field trip. Their goal was to plan a (4)_____ trip that
descriptive adjective

would give their classmates a sense of (5)_____. This
abstract singular noun

trip would be (6)_____ than last year's trip. In fact,
comparative adjective

this would be their (7)_____ field trip ever. It would
superlative adjective

give each classmate an opportunity to (8)_____,
present tense action verb

(9)_____, and (10)_____. The class would
present tense action verb   present tense action verb

travel (11)_____ mountains, (12)_____ tall
preposition   preposition

buildings, (13)_____ historical monuments,
preposition

(14)_____ (15)_____ rivers, and
preposition   descriptive adjective

(16)_____ the (17)_____ oceans. Besides all
preposition   descriptive adjective

this, they could photograph the many (18)_____ and
concrete plural noun

(19)_____ along the way.
concrete plural noun

Next the (20)_____ of classmates began working
collective noun

on the trip schedule. This (21)_____ journey would
descriptive adjective

begin at nine a.m. on Friday. When their teacher said that the

class would have to return by one p.m. that day for their

dictation test, the three classmates (22)_____ and
past tense action verb

frowned.

Add commas as needed to the following sentences.

1. Please come to my piano recital on May 10 2006 at the auditorium.

2. On Wednesday September 21 2005 I moved from my childhood home in Denver Colorado.

3. I moved to 517 Fox Lane Blazer Township New Jersey 07712.

4. Blanca and Cruz visit family in Boise Idaho every summer.

5. Kelly drove from Salem Oregon to Olympia Washington last week.

6. Luz's new address is 4750 Long Street Arcadia California 91006.

7. The Southwestern states include Arizona New Mexico Oklahoma and Texas.

8. Illinois Indiana Iowa and Kansas are some of the Midwest states.

9. States in the Northeast include Connecticut Delaware Maine Maryland Massachusetts and others.

10. In Alaska you can walk on a glacier paddle a kayak and photograph wildlife.

11. Ms. Tidbit wore a red blouse a green skirt a purple vest and pink cowboy boots.

12. She carried a bag of apples a poodle with bows in its fur and a half-eaten sandwich.

13. Please respond to my invitation by Monday September 19 2005.

14. I shall show you samples of igneous metamorphic and sedimentary rocks.

Add commas as needed to the following sentences.

1. Try my dear cousin to remember which goal belongs to the other team.

2. Ask me Wakefield if you have any questions.

3. Grandma where were you born?

4. Don't wake that sleeping tiger Uncle Robert!

5. Aunt Waverly have you ever seen an anteater?

6. Anteaters don't eat aunts my silly nephew!

7. Marsha Mellow Ph.D. has created new software for confection manufacturers.

8. Oscar Didit D.D. teaches religion and philosophy at the university.

9. Jaime Chávez M.B.A. became president of a large publishing company.

10. Did Duc Eng R.N. bandage your wounded knees?

11. Come back soon my friend for I'll miss you.

12. Dad have you seen my grammar book?

13. You left it out in the rain sweetheart.

14. I'm sorry Dad.

15. Mrs. Vega you might want to take Cornflower to Luis P. Bensen D.V.M. for her puppy shots.

16. Cornflower has already had her puppy shots Mary.

17. Did Charles B. Heale L.P.N. care for you at the hospital?

18. I've never met him Wassim.

Insert commas to offset the nonessential appositives in the sentences below.

1. Ogden Nash a famous poet wrote some hilarious limericks.

2. High-tech industries prosper in Raleigh the capital of North Carolina.

3. I asked my best friend Terrance if he knew my sister's best friend Wilda.

4. The oboe a woodwind instrument can sound sad.

5. *Pianissimo* an Italian word means "very quiet."

6. The French horn a brass instrument is shaped like a circle.

7. Tom plays the tuba the largest horn in the brass family.

8. Peter Tchaikovsky a Russian composer wrote *The Nutcracker* and many other ballets.

9. Richmond the capital of Virginia has some wonderful museums and theaters.

10. The capital of Kansas Topeka lies west of Kansas City.

11. Gutzon Borglum an amazing sculptor carved four Presidents in the Mount Rushmore National Memorial in South Dakota.

12. Wisconsin America's Dairyland is famous for its milk and cheese.

13. Abraham Lincoln our sixteenth President lived in Illinois for many years.

14. Have you seen Penelope my miniature rabbit?

15. She hasn't eaten her dinner two juicy carrots and some alfalfa.

Add commas to offset introductory and interrupting elements and afterthoughts.

1. Without a doubt that was the funniest story I've ever heard.

2. Max attended a ballet for the first time I believe last Friday night.

3. He had never seen people dance on their toes it seems.

4. The dancers of course were extremely athletic.

5. Their talent I thought was superb!

6. Max doesn't appreciate ballet I guess.

7. In my opinion his comment revealed his ignorance.

8. No he was not trying to be silly.

9. He said that they should have hired taller dancers of all things.

10. Yes I laughed out loud.

Underline the dependent clause in each sentence, and circle the subordinating conjunction.

1. Although he does not dance well, he has many other talents.

2. I have heard that he plays the oboe.

3. When she was six, she learned to swim.

4. If you turn left, you will come to the state Capitol building.

5. I shall not accept your money because bribery is unethical.

6. While John was elated at first, his elation did not last long.

7. An ornithologist might know where those eagles sleep.

8. Perhaps the meteorologist can tell us when the storm will hit.

9. Though he feigns bravery, he is frightened.

10. If the facts are pertinent, you may use them in your essay.

11. Since Eli was contrite, Ms. Hoo forgave him.

12. They call Raj a linguist because he speaks several languages.

Place commas where they are needed in these sentences.

1. David is a genteel industrious landscape artist.

2. When the boss arrived she found indolent disrespectful employees sitting around and sipping lemonade.

3. Lulu's superfluous bulky baggage slows her on the trip.

4. Because we had a helpful intuitive guide we made it safely through the dark dangerous jungle.

5. Before you were born an elderly benevolent man donated land for the park.

6. As soon as you finish we shall take a long pleasant drive through the countryside.

7. His wild ridiculous story was implausible.

8. If you can tolerate hot humid weather then you will enjoy Florida in the summer.

9. My sensible frugal aunt washed her paper plate and cup.

10. Her wealthy extravagant uncle threw away his fancy costly mug because it was dirty.

11. He gave me the valuable intangible gift of his time.

12. I had the momentary worrisome thought that it might rain on our parade.

Place commas where they are needed in these sentences.

1. Mom told me "Your great-grandparents' home was quaint and serene."

2. "I especially liked the potbellied stove" she said.

3. Wally shouted "Watch out for the poison ivy!"

4. She tripped and fell for the trail was steep and rocky.

5. Sue helped her up and I carried her backpack.

6. That sentence goes on and on but it is not redundant.

7. My sagacious friend studied hard yet she forgot the capital of Alaska.

8. Molly moaned "How could I have forgotten Juneau?"

9. Elle asked "What is the capital of Wyoming?"

10. "I think it's Cheyenne" said Kurt.

11. Elle was not sure so she looked at a map.

12. Elle said "I cannot find Shy Ann on the map."

Place quotation marks where they are needed in these sentences.

1. An ice pack might meliorate the swelling, said Dr. Lacy.

2. Juan asked, Is the melioration of swelling important?

3. Swelling, said Dr. Lacy, can cause discomfort.

4. Ms. Hoo said, Do not let prepositions daunt you.

5. Prepositions don't daunt me. It's the diagramming! cried Liz.

6. Keep trying, said Ms. Hoo, and you will learn.

7. I once knew a dauntless explorer, she said, who failed again and again.

8. Did he or she ever succeed? asked Liz.

9. Of course, said Ms. Hoo, but it took a long time.

10. Liz said, Long and complicated sentences confuse me.

11. Besides, she added, diagramming taxes my brain cells.

12. Diagramming, said Ms. Hoo, will strengthen those brain cells.

In the following sentences, enclose titles of songs and short literary works in quotation marks.

1. Ivy wrote a poem called Oh, to Be a Bird!

2. I titled my short story In the Nick of Time.

3. Josh Billings's essay, The Bumblebee, made people laugh.

4. A newspaper article called Paper Sculpture caught my eye.

5. All the way to Des Moines, they sang She'll be Comin' Round the Mountain.

6. Can you play Jingle Bells on the clarinet?

7. Professor Cruz gave a lecture titled How to Develop Good Study Habits.

8. Backpacking in the High Sierras is the magazine article that sparked my interest.

9. My friend titled her expository essay Safety Tips for Kayaking.

10. People began tapping their feet to the song Grandma's Feather Bed.

11. Please do not sing Found a Peanut again!

12. Max's poem, The Banana Slug, won first prize.

Underline all words that should be italicized in print.

1. Dad's favorite movie is The Music Man.

2. Quan reads The Rocky Mountain News every morning.

3. Have you seen the big musical production Pilgrim?

4. Caleb listens to a music CD called White Noise.

5. Someday I shall read Herman Melville's novel Moby Dick.

6. The aircraft carrier U.S.S. Constitution just left the harbor.

7. Karen named her sailboat the Pelican.

8. Have you seen Thomas Gainsborough's painting Blue Boy?

9. Max does not appreciate ballet, but he went to see The Nutcracker anyway.

10. Please use the word subvert in a sentence.

11. Its scientific name is Columba fasciata, but we call it a pigeon.

12. What does the Spanish word demasiado mean?

Complete this irregular verb chart by writing the past and past participle forms of each verb.

	VERB	PAST	PAST PARTICIPLE
1.	beat	_____	_____
2.	bite	_____	_____
3.	bring	_____	_____
4.	build	_____	_____
5.	burst	_____	_____
6.	buy	_____	_____
7.	catch	_____	_____
8.	come	_____	_____
9.	cost	_____	_____
10.	dive	_____	_____
11.	drag	_____	_____
12.	draw	_____	_____
13.	drown	_____	_____
14.	drive	_____	_____
15.	eat	_____	_____
16.	fall	_____	_____
17.	feel	_____	_____
18.	fight	_____	_____
19.	find	_____	_____
20.	flee	_____	_____
21.	fly	_____	_____
22.	forget	_____	_____
23.	forgive	_____	_____

Circle the correct verb form for each sentence.

1. Yesterday the Jays (beated, beat) the Doves in soccer.

2. The Jays have (beat, beaten) them in every tournament.

3. For yesterday's picnic, I (brang, brought) watermelon.

4. I have always (brung, brought) watermelon.

5. Last summer we (builded, built) a treehouse.

6. We have (builded, built) two treehouses.

7. Rob (buyed, bought) a plum tree.

8. He has (buyed, bought) three trees this week.

9. Len (catched, caught) a cold.

10. He has (catched, caught) a bad one.

11. Rachel (comed, came) home early.

12. She has (came, come) home to rest.

13. Last week, apples (costed, cost) 99¢ a pound.

14. They have (cost, costed) less in the past.

15. Melody (dove, dive) into the pool.

16. She has (dove, dived) in before.

17. I (drawed, drew) a happy face.

18. I have (drawed, drawn) several.

19. Leroy (drived, drove) to Kansas City.

20. He had (drove, driven) forty miles.

21. A limb (falled, fell) from the tree.

22. Limbs have (falled, fell, fallen) every year.

23. Tomcats (fighted, fought) last night.

24. They have (fighted, fought) every night this week.

25. A goose (flied, flew) by.

26. The geese have (flew, flown) south.

Complete this irregular verb chart by writing the past and past participle forms of each verb.

	VERB	PAST	PAST PARTICIPLE
1.	get	_____	_____
2.	give	_____	_____
3.	go	_____	_____
4.	hang (execute)	_____	_____
5.	hang (suspend)	_____	_____
6.	hide	_____	_____
7.	hold	_____	_____
8.	keep	_____	_____
9.	lay (place)	_____	_____
10.	lead	_____	_____
11.	lend	_____	_____
12.	lie (recline)	_____	_____
13.	lie (deceive)	_____	_____
14.	lose	_____	_____
15.	make	_____	_____
16.	mistake	_____	_____
17.	put	_____	_____
18.	ride	_____	_____
19.	rise	_____	_____
20.	run	_____	_____
21.	see	_____	_____
22.	sell	_____	_____

Choose the correct verb form for each sentence.

1. The docent (gived, gave) a tour of the Capitol.

2. He has (gived, gave, given) several tours today.

3. Ana (goed, went) to Scotland.

4. She has (went, gone) once before.

5. We (hanged, hung) a painting on the wall.

6. We have (hanged, hung) paintings and photos.

7. She (hided, hid) the pie from me!

8. He (holded, held) a fluffy kitten.

9. Tom has (keeped, kept) the secret.

10. Pam (layed, laid) her pen on the table.

11. She has (layed, laid) two books on the table.

12. She was tired, so she (laid, lay) on the sofa.

13. She has (laid, lain) there all afternoon!

14. George (losed, lost) his keys again.

15. He has (losed, lost) them twice before.

16. I (maked, made) a friend yesterday.

17. I have (maked, made) many friends.

18. Last night, I (putted, put) hand lotion on my toothbrush!

19. I have never before (putted, put) hand lotion on anything but my hands.

20. The sun (rised, rose) at 6 a.m.

21. It has (risen, rosen) earlier each morning.

22. I (seen, saw) him earlier.

23. I have (seen, saw) him every day.

24. She (selled, sold) her skates.

25. She has (selled, sold) two pairs of skates.

Complete this irregular verb chart by writing the past and past participle forms of each verb.

	VERB	PAST	PAST PARTICIPLE
1.	set	_____	_____
2.	shake	_____	_____
3.	shine (light)	_____	_____
4.	shine (polish)	_____	_____
5.	shut	_____	_____
6.	sit	_____	_____
7.	slay	_____	_____
8.	sleep	_____	_____
9.	spring	_____	_____
10.	stand	_____	_____
11.	strive	_____	_____
12.	swim	_____	_____
13.	swing	_____	_____
14.	take	_____	_____
15.	teach	_____	_____
16.	tell	_____	_____
17.	think	_____	_____
18.	wake	_____	_____
19.	weave	_____	_____
20.	wring	_____	_____
21.	write	_____	_____

Choose the correct verb form for each sentence.

1. Lulu (setted, set) the alarm.

2. She has (setted, set) it every night.

3. He (shook, shaked) her hand.

4. She has (shaked, shaken) many hands.

5. A light (shined, shone) through the window.

6. The light has (shined, shone) each evening.

7. Josh (shined, shone) his black shoes.

8. He has (shined, shone) several pairs of shoes.

9. Jan (shutted, shut) the window.

10. She has (shutted, shut) all the windows.

11. He (sitted, sat) on the bench.

12. He has (sitted, sat) there for two innings.

13. I (slept, sleeped) twelve hours.

14. Have you ever (slept, sleeped) that long?

15. She (standed, stood) in line.

16. She has (standed, stood) there before.

17. We (swam, swum) in the pool.

18. We have (swam, swum) many laps.

19. He (taked, took) his boa to the vet.

20. He has (took, taken) it to the vet twice this week.

21. Ilbea (teached, taught) me to sew.

22. She has (teached, taught) me many new skills.

23. Grace (telled, told) me a joke.

24. Has she (telled, told) you the joke?

25. I (thinked, thought) you were sagacious.

26. I have always (thinked, thought) that.

Circle each adverb in these sentences.

1. Yesterday the wind blew hard.

2. I felt somewhat grumpy, for it rudely destroyed my hairdo.

3. I have never heard a noise so loud.

4. It swept away my homework.

5. Then it stopped.

6. I had not quite finished my math.

7. I desperately gathered the papers together.

8. Will the wind blow again tomorrow?

9. Now it has calmed nicely.

10. Will I ever find all those papers?

11. I shall smooth my hair later.

12. I really think my homework has disappeared forever.

Replace commas with semicolons where they are needed in these sentences.

1. We shall pass through Denver, Colorado, Austin, Texas, and Memphis, Tennessee.

2. He plays the piano, she plays the drums, the flute, and the trumpet.

3. Carrots, celery, and peas are vegetables, apples, oranges, and bananas are fruits.

4. They have ants in their kitchen, moreover, termites are eating the door frame.

5. George washed the car, cleaned the house, and mowed the lawn, consequently, he fell asleep during the movie.

6. It snowed, therefore, I wore a jacket.

7. Gia and Allison will be there, also, Cecilia will come if she can.

8. Mae enjoys planting trees, for example, she planted two pines and an oak today.

9. Rita cleaned the garage, furthermore, she organized all the tools and boxes.

10. The sky was cloudy, nevertheless, we went to the park.

11. Ms. Hoo wore high heels, as a result, her feet hurt.

12. Would you rather visit Richmond, Virginia, Juneau, Alaska, or Phoenix, Arizona?

Insert apostrophes where they are needed in these sentences.

1. She couldnt remember whether shed been in Mexico in 88 or 89.

2. Mr. Collins yelled, "Good mornin!" to his neighbor.

3. "Oh my," exclaimed Mabel, "they were just walkin and talkin, and they never saw the bus leavin!"

4. Cant you see that I havent time to waste?

5. Didnt Mom graduate from high school with the class of 80?

6. Isnt her frugality obvious?

7. Were going to the library. Arent you?

8. Theyre going to the library also.

9. Wouldnt you like to join us?

10. Shell come if she can.

11. Well forgive her if she doesnt come.

12. We couldnt see through the foggy window.